NEW DIRECTIONS FOR HIGHER EDUCATION

Martin Kramer
EDITOR-IN-CHIEF

Leadership Transitions: The New College President

Judith Block McLaughlin
Graduate School of Education, Harvard University

EDITOR

Number 93, Spring 1996

JOSSEY-BASS PUBLISHERS
San Francisco

LEADERSHIP TRANSITIONS: THE NEW COLLEGE PRESIDENT
Judith Block McLaughlin (ed.)
New Directions for Higher Education, no. 93
Volume XXIV, Number 1
Martin Kramer, Editor-in-Chief

© 1996 by Jossey-Bass Inc., Publishers. All rights reserved.

No part of this issue may be reproduced in any form—except for a brief quotation (not to exceed 500 words) in a review or professional work—without permission in writing from the publishers.

Microfilm copies of issues and articles are available in 16mm and 35mm, as well as microfiche in 105mm, through University Microfilms Inc., 300 North Zeeb Road, Ann Arbor, Michigan 48106-1346.

ISSN 0271-0560   ISBN 0-7879-9872-9

NEW DIRECTIONS FOR HIGHER EDUCATION is part of The Jossey-Bass Higher and Adult Education Series and is published quarterly by Jossey-Bass Inc., Publishers, 350 Sansome Street, San Francisco, California 94104-1342. Second-class postage paid at San Francisco, California, and at additional mailing offices. POSTMASTER: Send address changes to New Directions for Higher Education, Jossey-Bass Inc., Publishers, 350 Sansome Street, San Francisco, California 94104-1342.

SUBSCRIPTIONS for 1996 cost $50.00 for individuals and $72.00 for institutions, agencies, and libraries.

EDITORIAL CORRESPONDENCE should be sent to the Editor-in-Chief, Martin Kramer, 2807 Shasta Road, Berkeley, California 94708-2011.

Cover photograph and random dot by Richard Blair/Color & Light © 1990.

Manufactured in the United States of America on Lyons Falls Pathfinder Tradebook. This paper is acid-free and 100 percent totally chlorine-free.

Contents

EDITOR'S NOTES 1
Judith Block McLaughlin

1. Entering the Presidency 5
Judith Block McLaughlin
Leadership transitions are stressful for both the new president and the institution, but successful management of transitions can increase the likelihood of an effective presidential tenure.

2. Establishing Key Relationships 15
Roger H. Martin
A new president shares his thoughts and feelings in the early days of his tenure as he learns about his job and develops relationships with key constituents.

3. Surviving and Thriving 25
Sue A. Cox
In the chaos and excitement of the city, the president of a newly decentralized community college tackles the many challenges of reorganization, including making programmatic decisions, finding necessary resources, and developing support from the community.

4. Confronting Value Conflicts 33
Paul G. Risser
The name of a university's athletic teams is considered racist and insensitive by some, while to others it reflects great pride. The new president must reconcile these conflicting values.

5. Assuming the Bully Pulpit 41
Rita Bornstein
Results of a survey of college presidents indicate when and why presidents take public positions on public policy issues, and illuminate the complexities of the president's role as public intellectual.

6. Finding a Balance 51
Milton A. Gordon, Margaret F. Gordon
In the midst of the all-consuming schedule of the presidency, new presidents must find some way to retain control over their lives.

7. Developing a Vision   59
Claire Gaudiani
New presidents can draw on the folk story "Stone Soup" for a model of how they can work with their institutional community to develop a common vision.

8. Demystifying the Presidency   71
Robert Hahn
The ideal president does not exist, and our mythic thinking obscures a serious consideration of how we can create the conditions for more successful leadership for our colleges and universities.

9. Afterword: Reflections on the College Presidency   85
David Riesman
The college presidency is a job with unanticipated hazards and happy discoveries, says one of the foremost authorities on higher education.

INDEX   88

Editor's Notes

During the past fifteen years, I have had the privilege of talking with literally hundreds of new college, university, and community college presidents while pursuing research on leadership transitions and chairing the Harvard Seminar for New Presidents. I have spoken with these new presidents about their decisions to consider the presidency and their experiences as candidates. I have asked them about their thoughts and feelings as they assume the office: their expectations, aspirations, excitement, and fears. And I have heard about the surprises they have encountered, the issues and obstacles they have faced, and the exasperations and delights of their jobs.

I have come away from these conversations convinced of several things. First, for both the new presidents and their institutions, the presidential leadership transition is an intense experience, which has serious ramifications for the success of the president's tenure. Second, far too little explicit attention is given to this period of entry. Ironically, although considerable time is spent orienting new students to our institutions, little thought is devoted to designing an orientation or entry process for our senior leadership. Third, there is a great deal of wisdom about leadership transitions to be gleaned from presidents themselves.

This sourcebook emanates from these conclusions. It describes some of the experiences of new presidents during their leadership transition, addresses the varying issues and dilemmas new presidents encounter, and offers advice based on research and first-hand experience. The perspectives included herein are intentionally diverse, in recognition that, just as there is no one generic community college, college, or university in the United States, neither is there a generic presidency. Each presidential post and each leadership transition is unique, a particular concatenation of individual president, institutional context, and historical moment. The analysis and recommendations presented here must be interpreted with regard to the specific circumstances of a particular leadership transition. This volume is written for new presidents and more experienced presidents, for individuals who aspire to the presidency, and for those who work with new presidents and have a stake in seeing them succeed.

Chapter One draws on my research on leadership transitions, examining the issues and pressures newcomers face in launching their presidencies, and assessing why new presidents find the job of president qualitatively different from positions they have previously held. Chapter One describes the position of the new president, identifies several reasons presidents fail, and suggests ways to increase the likelihood of a successful entry into the presidency.

Chapter Two is an excerpt from the journal of a new president. When Roger Martin accepted the presidency of Moravian College, David Riesman and I suggested that he keep a journal of his early days in office. Many presidents begin with this intention, but find that the demands of the presidency make sustaining the effort impossible. Roger Martin persisted, and his journal provides a fascinating glimpse into the everyday life of the new president, conveying his thoughts and feelings in the early days of his tenure. The selection included here describes his first meetings with senior staff, faculty, and trustees, as he undertook what is perhaps the most important task of a new president, the development of effective working relationships with key constituents.

In Chapter Three, we are transported to an altogether different presidential context from the small, private college world of Roger Martin. Shortly after Sue Cox, president of Southwestern College, attended the 1992 Harvard Seminar for New Presidents, she wrote me of her reactions as she compared her situation at the Houston Community College System with that of her presidential colleagues in the seminar:

> I heard discussions about the need for diversification and how one best does it, and I thought about the struggle to deal with the needs of an already diversified population whose skills are woefully inadequate and who only have one last chance to make it—whose struggle is not about rights but about access to a system that seems increasingly remote. I heard discussions about capital campaigns for museums, etc., and I thought about how to get the carpet replaced in one of our converted warehouse campuses. I heard about the culture of an institution and wondered how to know and deal with it in eleven centers across a geographical area of 40 miles. I heard about the jealously guarded rights and privileges of faculty and wondered how I could find the space to provide our faculty with offices other than the trunks of their cars. I heard discussions about the dangers of making too many transfers from endowment funds and wondered if my small budget contingency would get us through the year without a crisis. We are at root a college whose mission places it on the front lines of the struggle to stay ahead of catastrophe in this country. Our faculty is committed, even beyond reason and when it seems it isn't doable, to teaching the huge array of people who come in our doors. Our facilities are lousy but what goes on in our classrooms isn't.

In Chapter Three, Sue Cox speaks passionately about the mission of institutions that "do their work amidst the chaos and excitement of our cities," and reveals the difficulties faced by a president who is attempting to help her institution simultaneously survive and thrive.

One of the most daunting challenges facing presidents today is having to make institutional policy in the midst of differing—and sometimes irreconcilable—values about diversity. New presidents are especially vulnerable to having such issues raised; their arrival often serves as an opening in which controversial issues emerge. Such was the case for Paul Risser. Shortly after beginning his tenure at Miami University, he was confronted with the question of whether to retain or to reject the name of the University sports teams, the Redskins. A controversial issue for any institution, Miami's situation was complicated by the University's long-standing relationship with the Miami Tribe, whence the institution got its name. Paul Risser's situation was complicated by the fact that he was a brand-new president whose every action received close scrutiny. In Chapter Four, Paul Risser explains why he chose to face this issue head-on and delineates the process he employed to do so, and then retrospectively examines the benefits and costs of his decisions.

Chapter Five expands this discussion of "taking a stand" by examining the question of whether presidents should take a public position on partisan and other heated policy issues. Rita Bornstein, president of Rollins College, became interested in this question early in her presidency when she was asked to become involved in political campaigns and take positions on issues of public policy. Curious to learn of the judgments of other presidents regarding if and when to take public positions, Rita Bornstein conducted a survey of independent college presidents. She presents her findings in Chapter Five and discusses why assuming the bully pulpit is so difficult both for new and experienced presidents.

In the inaugural year of the Harvard Seminar for New Presidents, one session was entitled "the personal side of the presidency." One president, who had been in office for several months, quipped, "You mean there is some personal time?" In Chapter Six, Milton Gordon, president of California State University, Fullerton, and an alumnus of that first Harvard Seminar, and his wife, Margaret Gordon, dean of extended education at California State University, Dominguez Hills, share their reflections about how to preserve personal time and privacy in the midst of the very public and all-consuming job of the presidency.

Chapter Six employs both the first-person singular and plural pronouns. "I" is used when referring to the president; "we" is used in discussing the couple. Throughout the chapter, however, the ideas and insights are the contributions of both authors. This shift in pronouns reflects an important and highly complicated reality of the college presidency. The job is filled by one person, to whom is directed an almost inordinate amount of attention. Yet, even in this era of two-career couples, the presidency is, in many respects, a "two-for" position, both in terms of the expectations about the spouse's participation and in terms of the impact of the presidency on the life of the president's family.

Chapter Seven examines the responsibility of the new president for articulating a vision for their institutions. Paradoxically, new presidents are asked to state their vision at the very time when they know the least about the institution they are heading. Claire Gaudiani draws upon her experience as president of Connecticut College to suggest a plan whereby new presidents can simultaneously learn about their new institution and work with the diverse institutional constituents to develop a mutual understanding of institutional prospects and possibilities.

If the responsibilities of the presidency sit too heavily on an individual's shoulders, Chapter Eight provides an important antidote. Robert Hahn, president of Johnson State College, recommends that we demystify presidential leadership. Presently, our colleges and universities search for some unattainable "Ideal President," and are fooled into believing that such a person could actually exist. Hence, there is inevitable disappointment when the individual appointed turns out to be human after all. Robert Hahn analyzes some of the common myths about presidential leadership and offers a new formulation that shifts the concept of success from an individual to a collective responsibility.

This sourcebook closes with an Afterword by David Riesman, professor emeritus at Harvard University and long-time observer of the college presidency. During the past sixty years, he has spoken and corresponded with literally thousands of presidents about wide-ranging matters in their lives, from personal concerns to professional issues. Indeed, he can properly take credit for a great many appointments; David Riesman has undoubtedly written far more letters of nomination and recommendation for prospective presidents than anyone else. In this volume, he offers his reflections on the college presidency, sharing his wisdom with yet another generation of new presidents.

A great many people are owed thanks for their contributions to the research and writing of this sourcebook. I am grateful to Martin Kramer, the New Directions for Higher Education editor-in-chief, who invited me to take on this project and provided wise counsel and helpful assistance throughout. I am grateful to the presidents who contributed outstanding work, on schedule, to this volume, agreeing to accept this assignment, despite the fact that they already had far more to do than humanly possible. They demonstrate the truth of the bromide: when you want something done, ask a busy person. Special thanks are due to David Riesman, who provided me an extraordinary private tutorial on higher education during our research on the college presidency, presidential searches, and Open Meeting and Open Record laws.

This volume could not have been written without conversations with hundreds of new and experienced presidents about their lives and their work. I am grateful to all these presidents for sharing their experiences and insights.

Judith Block McLaughlin
Editor

JUDITH BLOCK MCLAUGHLIN chairs the Harvard Seminar for New Presidents. She is director of the field experience program and lecturer on higher education at the Harvard University Graduate School of Education.

Like a diver poised at the end of a diving board, the new president can make a graceful dive or do a belly flop during the period of entry into the presidency.

Entering the Presidency

Judith Block McLaughlin

To describe the mind-set of the college or university president embarking on his or her first presidency, I often use the analogy of a person standing at the end of the high diving board for the first time. This person has probably dived off lower-level boards many times before, and has mounted the ladder to the high dive enthusiastically and energetically, eager to take on this new level of skill and thrill. Yet, as anyone knows who has ever stood at the end of a high diving board, the water below seems very deep and very far away. For the diver now sees not only the surface of the water, but all the way down to the bottom of the deep end of the swimming pool.

At that moment, poised to dive, the diver feels both excitement and fear. While realizing that the sensation of soaring through the air can be exhilarating, the diver is also aware that this flight can be frightening. The possibility of a belly flop looms. And not only will an awkward dive draw attention because of the size of splash (whereas a smooth dive will go largely unnoticed), a belly flop off the high dive can be painful.

New presidents find themselves in much the same situation as this diver. Although the great majority of presidents have risen through the ranks of academic administration, and the remainder have been appointed because they have demonstrated talent and skills in other arenas, in assuming the college or university presidency they are taking on a greater challenge, with both increased opportunities and heightened personal risks. They were selected as presidents precisely because they had been successful. Yet, as new presidents, they find themselves at much greater risk for failure than ever before in their careers. For, as they certainly realize, many presidents are not beloved, and some leave their posts not entirely by choice.

Furthermore, postpresidential appointments can be difficult to find. Whereas vice presidents or deans—no matter how lackluster their performance—can usually locate other positions, in moves up, down, or sidewise, ex-presidents find their prospects more severely constrained. Presidents who are perceived to have failed (or, almost as damaging, to have been controversial) will find most doors to other presidencies closed. Even a return to the vice presidential level is often difficult to negotiate, as many college presidents are reluctant to hire a former president out of concern that this person will behave like he or she still is the chief executive.

But if the risks facing new presidents are daunting, the prospective pleasures of the job beckon. For most new presidents, the presidential post represents the pinnacle of a career. Although it is not a job prospect they entertained until well along in their careers (after all, not many grammar school youngsters answer "college president" to the question of what they want to be when they grow up), the job of president, once considered, becomes increasingly enticing. It represents an opportunity to assume responsibility for an entire educational enterprise, to make a difference in a world which they value. As the presidents who have contributed to this volume attest, the presidency is an invigorating, rewarding, and always interesting post.

Presidents face their new venture, then, not unaware of the perils before them, but eager for this challenge. The institutions that receive them have similarly mixed reactions. In the first part of this chapter, we will note what is at stake for each partner in this interplay between individual and institution. Next, we examine several reasons presidencies sometimes don't work, examining the most common causes of belly flops. Finally, we will identify some practices that can increase the likelihood of presidential success. The data for this chapter are drawn from formal interviews, informal conversations, and correspondence with new presidents and the trustees and campus constituents who work with them.

New Partnership

For new presidents, the period from their first consideration of the presidential post through the first year in office is a time of considerable adjustment. New presidents must adjust to the new role, acclimate themselves and their families to new surroundings, and acquaint themselves with the institution and its diverse personnel. There is no shortage of people willing and eager to advise them; but the new presidents don't yet know whose advice to trust. Similarly, new presidents do not lack things to do; their calendars fill up all by themselves if the presidents don't intervene. Yet, how do they judge what is important, what deserves the *president's* time and attention and what events or items do not require their presence or involvement?

Even if new presidents come from inside the institution, the presidency gives them a new vantage point and perspective. As Marjorie Bakken, president of Wheelock College, explained in a memorandum to her senior staff early in her first year:

I have been a member of the Wheelock community for 25 years. Yet my new role as president makes this a transition year for me and, consequently, to some degree, for many other people at Wheelock. For me, the challenge of the transition lies in listening responsively in new ways to messages and voices I may have heard before. Transitions are both smooth and bumpy. The smoothness lies in the familiarity and the support and encouragement from the community. The roughness comes from my newness at making certain decisions, my changing perceptions of the College and the community's changing perception of me in a new role. [M. Bakken, Wheelock College memorandum, Sept. 1993]

In our conversations, new presidents have reported many surprises during their first year in office. These include surprise at the nature of the president's job—the pace one must keep, the number and range of demands, and the issues brought to the president's attention. Others concern the institution itself; as with any new relationship, there is a great deal to be learned and some of the initial impressions, assumptions, and assurances disappear under closer scrutiny. Finally, many of the surprises are related to the fact that the post of president differs in many ways from any other job in academe.

Although new presidents have previously held demanding jobs and many have worked closely with other presidents, they report surprise, even shock, at the schedules and pace of their first year in office. The job is "extremely stimulating, but it's also exhausting. I am going to have to learn to pace myself," commented one new president after a few months in office. Said another: "A *normal* pace is in fact very *abnormal* in terms of human need and endurance." The extraordinarily long hours, filled with an unrelenting series of appointments and appearances and an overflowing in-basket, mean that the president must always be "on"; there is little time for reflection, much less for self-renewal. The problem of managing a schedule is exacerbated by the fact that during the first year in office, the new president is under pressure, both external and self-imposed, to be everywhere, to take advantage of every opportunity to learn more about the institution, to meet key constituents, to see and be seen. The situation is complicated because, in the absence of knowing what the new "boss" wants sent his or her way, senior administrators and others err in the direction of sending everything to the new president. In Thomas North Gilmore (1988, p. 138) calls this phenomenon the "cycle of overloading the leader," noting that it is especially common in the early days of new administrative relationships. Hence, new presidents find that they are asked to deal with an extraordinary number of topics, ranging, as Arthur Rothkopf, president of Lafayette College, commented in his inaugural speech on October 21, 1994, "from lofty issues of institutional policy and strategic planning to only slightly less urgent matters concerning beer kegs and flex dollars."

Still other surprises for new presidents have to do with situations and issues they discover at their institution. Although these surprises differ from place to place, the lament of the new president is the same: "Nobody told me about . . ." or "They didn't let on how serious the situation really was." Sometimes, the bad news (for it is invariably bad news that wasn't shared!) was not conveyed to the new president prior to his or her arrival on campus because the institution wanted to present its best face in the courting process so as to attract the most attractive prospect. This is a not uncommon but unfortunate behavior, which results in the new president, quite understandably, feeling misled or outright deceived (McLaughlin and Riesman, 1990, p. 300). Not infrequently, presidents discover that senior administrators in their cabinet had sought the presidency and are displeased at being passed over for the job. Sometimes, the "things that no one told me" were not shared because the board of trustees did not know about them. Thus, the new president is placed in the unenviable position of having to be the one to relay the bad news to the institution.

By far the greatest surprises have to do with the realization that the presidency, unlike any other position in higher education, is not simply a job. It is a role that defines how an individual is perceived by others. New presidents enjoy the veneration that greets them on their arrival, and they are stunned by the vilification that also inevitably comes. Despite the fact that higher education is essentially anti-authoritarian, the focus is on the president. The president speaks not as an individual but as the representative of the institution.

David Riesman has put it succinctly—presidents serve as the "living logo" of their institution. This symbolic role is both a heady and a burdensome proposition. Referring to the headiness, one new president commented, "I am still working on the task of determining who exactly I am in this new presidential role, in getting my ego under control." But the burden is also substantial. The president cannot delegate the symbolic role. The presence of the president lends an aura of legitimacy, even significance, to an event. In Chapter Four, Paul Risser describes an open forum at Miami University during which individuals expressed their arguments and passions concerning the question of the athletic teams' name, the Redskins. Risser stayed at the forum for the entire day, a sizable commitment of a president's time. In so doing, he made a powerful statement that this issue, and the diversity of opinion about it, mattered to him, and to the institution.

For many new presidents, it comes as a surprise that their words are taken far more seriously than they ever imagined. Many have reported having to curtail their typical "extrovert" (to borrow a word from the Meyers-Briggs inventory of types) style of thinking aloud. What they say, no matter how wistful or quixotic, is perceived as the president's, and thus the institution's, policy. New presidents learn quickly that they can no longer speak and act only as individuals. To many people, the president *is* the institution.

Campus Perspective

The experiences of the first year make the leadership transition both exciting and stressful for new presidents. This period is also exciting and stressful for the other people connected with the institution. The status quo has been disrupted, and the old rules do not necessarily apply. There is a sense of instability, as individuals wonder if they will be winners or losers under the new regime. Who will be "in" and who will be "out"? Even for those whose tenure is secure, the changing political alliances and the maneuvering for position and power are disruptive factors. The new environment affects everyone in the institution.

The arrival of a new president necessarily means change for an institution. However, the exact innovations, emendations, or permutations that will result from the new leadership are unpredictable. And since on every campus, many different visions of the institution compete for hegemony, campus constituents experience both hope and wariness.

In the absence of information about who the new president is and how he or she will behave, people try to read their new leader. One president reported that, despite the fact that she repeatedly told people on her campus that "her agenda was to work together with the state college to build a mutual agenda," many people did not believe her and suspected that she had her own strategic plan tucked into her back pocket. "She may say that she doesn't have an agenda yet, but does she *really* mean that?" Another president's request to be given a list of faculty committees was questioned; his appearance at a philosophy department colloquium was variously interpreted. Did this signify his interest in philosophy, which could be good news for that department, or did it suggest that he was looking at the department with an eye to budget cuts or reductions-in-force? The new president is observed and interpreted, and these perceptions and interpretations develop a meaning and reality of their own. As experienced presidents know all too well, "hearsay realities" have a real life; that is, the rumor is often much more powerful in its impact and duration than the actual facts.

Early Exits

The new president's tenure starts with great excitement and anticipation. Happily, in the great majority of cases, new presidents develop support for themselves and their ideas, and are able to establish effective partnerships with their institutions. But, occasionally, the presidency does not work out, and the president exits early from office.

These early exits are costly, both to the individuals and to the institutions who suffer them. Over the past decade, I have studied these presidential departures in an effort to understand what has caused them. Although each situation is unique and complex, defying easy characterization, most early exits appear to fall into three categories: appropriateness of the choice of president for an institution, events occurring at an institution, or relationships between the president and others.

I call the first category of early exits "admissions mistakes" or "rejection of alien tissue." The president's departure typically occurs within the first eighteen months and is traumatic for all concerned. It results from an inappropriate selection, the appointment either of a person who should not be a president, or, more often, of a person who does not belong at that particular institution.

In the first instance, the mismatch of person and presidential office, it is discovered that someone who has performed capably in other posts nevertheless lacks the talents, skills, or personality required for the presidency. As discussed earlier, the president's job differs significantly from other jobs; thus, a strong performance in a previous position does not guarantee success as president.

More often, however, the early exits in this category result from a perceived mismatch between the new president and the institutional setting. It is not that the new president is a failure, per se; rather it is that the individual seemingly does not fit the particular context. The mismatch usually becomes obvious quickly; the appointment is a graft that simply won't take.

Sometimes these mismatches are the result of faulty searches. In the courting process, the information gathered about the candidate, or the information shared with the candidate about the institution, was insufficient. If either party had known more, the disparities would have been apparent. But, ironically, not infrequently these mismatches were intentional—the new president was chosen precisely because he or she represented significant change. In the abstract, the change seemed highly desirable; in reality, it was disastrous. The institution comes to appreciate the aphorism: "Be careful what you ask for, for you may get it."

The second category of early exits can be called scapegoating or—in Thomas North Gilmore's phrase—"industrial accidents." Here, an event at the college or university propels the individual out of the presidency. Even though the crisis may not be of the president's making, he or she becomes the fall guy—the person forced to shoulder the blame.

In difficult situations, there is a human need to affix responsibility. Because of their prominent position, presidents are invariably made the scapegoats when things go awry. New presidents are especially at risk if they do not have a well-developed base of support that allows them to survive the assault.

I call the third category of early exits "irreconcilable differences" or "the accumulation of straws." These are also common reasons for departures much later in the presidency. Rather than the dramatic explosions often found in the first two categories of early exits, these departures result from the gradual accretion of small, unresolved grievances. Although the precipitating event may appear relatively minor and the campus or trustee reaction far out of proportion, it is the final straw for the institution, which has been displeased with the president for some time.

"I didn't see it coming. I had no idea there was such dissatisfaction with my performance," remarked one president in a lament not uncommon among presidents whose exits fall into this category. Because the new president and the board wanted to get along well, small concerns and dissatisfactions had remained unexpressed. Over time they accumulated until the differences were too many and too long-standing to be easily reconciled.

Smoother Entry

While failed presidencies, especially early exits, draw considerable attention, smoother passages receive considerably less notice. Yet the differences between the belly flops and the graceful dives are revealing. When examined closely, smooth entries typically include certain practices that have helped the new presidents establish themselves in their new position and have laid the groundwork for effective institutional leadership. These include an explicit entry plan, a reasonable pace of change, a few priorities for presidential action for the first year, and the development of key relationships.

From the moment of accepting the offer of the presidency, the new president is expected to make presidential decisions and appearances. New presidents' calendars are full even before they set foot on the campus; included are many requests for presidential action. Some of these requests are new proposals; others are ideas that the previous incumbent never acted upon; still others are problems that seem to require immediate attention. And because new presidents have been effective problem solvers and decision makers in their past positions, they feel the urge to plunge headlong into this arena of action.

But the reality is that they do not yet know enough to make informed decisions. They are not well acquainted with current practices, are not fully apprised of alternative options, and cannot adequately assess the consequences of new policies.

In a study of second-time presidents, Estela Bensimon reports that experienced presidents were more likely than first-time presidents to get to know their institutions before "making any pronouncements." They "approached learning about their institutions more aggressively and more systematically" (Bensimon, 1989, p. 2). Many successful first-time presidents do likewise. They design a carefully constructed plan to learn about their new institution. They do not just assume that getting acquainted will happen "along the way," or can be dispensed with in a few introductory meetings with administrators and faculty groups. Their plan for transition is intentional and explicit. That is, they think carefully about how they want to learn about their new institution and they explain this process to their governing board and campus. Additionally, as they listen and learn, they share their observations and insights and test their emerging theories with others. (For a comprehensive entry plan, see Cheever, 1982. Developed for a school superintendency, this same process also served Cheever well when he assumed the presidency of Wheelock College and the interim presidency of Simmons College.)

Some new presidents have initially reacted with strong reservations to the suggestion that they set aside a considerable amount of time to enacting an entry plan. "I don't have the time to wander around; I am expected to hit the ground running," said one president, while another wondered if the board and campus would "see me as not doing anything." New presidents who have successfully implemented entry plans have found that these have been well received when the board and institution understand the purpose of this transition period, participate in drafting the transition plan, and take part in discussions about what the president is learning about the institution. A carefully planned an executed entry becomes the new president's first act of leadership.

Of course some presidential decisions have to be made right away; some problems have to be addressed early on. But there are probably far fewer of these than may first appear. As part of the planned entry, the president, in conjunction with the senior staff and board, can identify which of the many items on the presidential agenda are of highest priority. The temptation is to make this a long list; the hard work is in being selective, in reducing the longer wish list to a few essential items.

New presidents will want to communicate these priorities to the campus and to ensure that the board agrees that these are, indeed, the items of highest priority. There is nothing worse for a new president or a veteran than to discover at the time of the board's evaluation that the president's list of priorities is at variance with the list on which the board is making its judgment about presidential performance!

Keeping focused on these few priorities helps the president and others to avoid a common pitfall of the first year—attempting to take on too much. New presidents report that among their hardest decisions are those having to do with the appropriate pace and timing of change. How fast should changes be made? When should new programs, personnel changes, reorganizations, and so on be introduced? My research suggests that new presidents are at greater risk of moving too rapidly than of proceeding too cautiously.

New presidents are often confronted with what appears to be an outright contradiction: on the one hand, they experience strong calls for presidential action; on the other hand, they encounter considerable resistance when they heed these calls. On closer examination, this paradox is explained by recognizing that administrators and faculty members are insecure and anxious about what change will mean, and hence are reluctant to give up the familiar, no matter how dysfunctional. Institutions, like people, can only absorb so much change at a time, no matter how desirable the change might be. In some of the cases where new presidents have lost their jobs because of a bad fit, this leadership casualty has probably been caused as much by the rapidity of change attempted by the new president as by the content of the changes or the person of the president. The president has badly misjudged the pace of change that was reasonable for the college or university.

Decisions such as the appropriate pace of change or the identification of priorities obviously cannot be made by a president in isolation. Hence, a critically important task of the presidential transition is the development of relationships with key institutional players. In higher education, relationships are the coin of the realm; the president's authority (and security) comes not from raw power but from the strength of his or her relationships with others at the institution. One of the ironies of presidential transition is that the new president supervises people who know far more about the college or university than the new president, but they defer to the president out of respect and insecurity. Thus, the responsibility falls to the new president to take the lead in becoming better acquainted with the expertise of staff members and their former modus operandi as individuals and as a group, and to discuss with them their new leader's preferred working style. In so doing, the president models the desired behavior of communication. Presidents who have made it clear early on that they value feedback are less likely to be overwhelmed later by an accumulation of straws of discontent. They are also more likely to have supporters who assist them in weathering the inevitable storms. As veteran presidents know well, while it is difficult to build trust, it is even more difficult to overcome distrust once it has been engendered.

This chapter began with the analogy of the new president as a diver standing alone at the end of a high diving board. Indeed, in many cases, the new president is left alone to find the way in the transition. Members of the search committee, pleased with the choice they have made, return to the responsibilities they put on hold during the extraordinarily time-consuming search process. Members of the governing board, equally happy to have the search concluded successfully, look to the new president to take charge.

But new presidents do not have to remain alone. Those presidents who work with their boards and campuses to make their entry to the presidency a time of active learning for themselves and their institutions find that they have accomplished a great deal in this transition period. In the process, they have adopted a style that allows for learning, one that will serve them well throughout their presidential tenure.

References

Bensimon, E. M., "Five Approaches to Think About: Lessons Learned from Experienced Presidents." In E. M. Bensimon, M. L. Gade, and J. F. Kauffman, *On Assuming a College or University Presidency*. Washington, D.C.: American Association for Higher Education, 1989.

Cheever, D. "A Good Beginning as a Superintendent." In B. Jentz and J. Wofford (eds.), *Entry*. Chestnut Hill, Mass.: Leadership and Learning, 1982.

Gilmore, T. N. *Making a Leadership Change: How Organizations and Leaders Can Handle Leadership Transitions Successfully*. San Francisco: Jossey-Bass, 1988.

McLaughlin, J. B., and Riesman, D. *Choosing a College President*. Princeton, N.J., Carnegie Foundation for the Advancement of Teaching, 1990.

JUDITH BLOCK MCLAUGHLIN chairs the Harvard Seminar for New Presidents. She is director of the field experience program and lecturer on higher education at the Harvard University Graduate School of Education.

This excerpt from one new president's journal identifies many of the tasks and challenges that greet new presidents in the early days of their tenure.

Establishing Key Relationships

Roger H. Martin

Little has been written about what happens to new presidents when they first arrive on campus. This is because for most of us, the first few chaotic weeks are a blur in our memories. It is difficult to recall the first words we uttered, let alone what we actually did when we first assumed office. I came to the college presidency, however, with the zeal of an inquisitive journalist. I had been a president's assistant at Middlebury College in one of my early incarnations and therefore was already a student of the U.S. college presidency. Moreover, as a Quaker with a hallowed tradition of journal-keeping to uphold, I was rather easily persuaded by David Reisman and Judith McLaughlin, my colleagues at Harvard where I was a dean, to keep a record of my first year as president of Moravian College in Bethlehem, Pennsylvania. Between September 1, 1986, and Commencement Day on May 31, 1987, I religiously recorded the peaks and troughs of a college president's existence—including successes and failures, fears and triumphs. What follows, then, is a candid accounting, drawn from the early parts of my journal, of what happens to most of us when we first take on this crazy job. Thrown in for good measure are some of my particular (some might say peculiar) views of the college president's first few weeks.

My feelings the first day as president of Moravian College ranged between awe and wonder—awe, because I was taking on enormous responsibilities for a venerable institution and many people; wonder, because I had achieved the status of college president at a relatively young age. This foolishness, however, caused me to make several naive assumptions. First, I assumed that everyone would know who I was when I arrived on campus. As we shall see, far from being an instant celebrity, I was more like a nonperson when I began my presidency. Furthermore, I expected that my commands, like those of a master sergeant, would be dutifully obeyed by the troops. I quickly discovered that a college is not an army! Finally, and perhaps most discouraging, I erroneously believed that change could be effected quickly. Colleges and universities are like the Mississippi River: Their course can be changed, but only after a great deal of patience and hard work. And even then, one always has to worry that they will go right back to where they were before the new president arrived.

The first assumption, then, is that as new presidents we have a visible identity. One could only wish that this were true, because it would save us from some extremely embarrassing situations. Unfortunately, quite the reverse is the case. Most of us did not campaign for the job, so even our primary constituencies—faculty, staff, and students—might not know what we look like when we first arrive on campus. Nor does our appearance give us away. Unlike politicians—with their full heads of hair, nice suntans, and perpetual smiles—most forty-year-old male college presidents tend to look like everyone else. We wear Hushpuppies and tweed sports jackets with arm patches. We drive modest automobiles and smoke pipes. In fact, we look just like the faculty! Only later do premature balding, bags under the eyes, and that haggard, hungry look distinctively set us apart from our colleagues.

For example, just before classes began I attended the semester's opening of Payne Gallery, an art facility that we are extremely proud of in Bethlehem. In the company of some of Bethlehem's most prominent citizens, I was left alone most of the evening gazing at the artwork and sipping warm white wine while everyone else enjoyed conversations in closely knit social groups. They weren't being rude. They simply did not know who I was because no one on my staff had thought to make the appropriate introductions. Of course, the reverse is not true. There is a general assumption, held largely by alumni and local citizens, that because we have Ph.D.'s and, more important, because we have risen to the top of the academic profession, new presidents have photographic memories and an intuitive ability to know by name, and without ever being introduced, all the important people in our various constituencies. And of course they all consider themselves to be important!

My meeting with the local aristocracy in Payne Gallery was only the first of several embarrassing encounters with the larger Bethlehem community, suggesting to my wife Susan and me that while very few people knew who we were, we were expected to know them. Several days after the gallery opening, I found a self-delivered letter in my mailbox from a well-known citizen complaining that not only had I ignored him at the reception (he apparently *did* know who I was), but that twice I had passed him on the street without even smiling!

The recognition factor was also a problem with students. Shortly after addressing the freshmen at Convocation on September 2 with what I thought was a brilliant and compelling speech, I found myself attending a dinner with a group of freshman scholarship recipients. Arriving late, I took the first available seat. The students at the table I selected were deeply engrossed in conversation. They did not even acknowledge my sudden appearance. Sensing that my convocation presentation had not made a great impact and that indeed the students I had joined for dinner maybe didn't recognize me, I puffed up my courage and introduced myself. "Hi. I'm Roger Martin, president of Moravian College! What are your names?" There was some awkward silence followed by the continuation of the previous conversation about a network of complex teenage relationships between two rival high schools, both represented by at least six students at the table. As far as they were concerned, I was a nonperson. But I persisted. "Tell me. What do you plan to major in?" This initiative at civilized conversation was met with icy stares. They would have nothing to do with my impertinent intrusion. Instead, the subject switched to the senior proms they had all attended not too many months before. They were probably embarrassed to be in the presence of an authority figure, someone who vaguely resembled their ancient parents. On the other hand, it probably still hadn't registered who I was. My ego, not to mention my pride, was mortally wounded.

By the end of September, things had improved. Wealthy widows living in town could spot me a mile away and duck into obscure alleyways as I approached, fearing that, as president, I might recruit them for a bequest. I was recognized by some other groups as well. Local charities knew me because they wanted the name of Moravian's president on their letterheads. And some irate alumni acknowledged my existence because of outrageous statements I had made about changing the college (in their opinion, in a negative direction). But even by late October, the campus police dispatcher did not yet know who the president of Moravian College was.

Every college has its traditions. One at Moravian is a ceremony that goes back to the early 1920s. Near midnight, pledges from a certain fraternity come over to Main Hall, a women's residence hall located next to the president's house, to serenade the women in front of perhaps two hundred onlookers. At some point, the women on the second floor dump a bucket of cold water on the serenaders and then everyone goes home. The problem was that nobody told Susan or me about this ancient tradition.

The appointed hour came. Up late working, I heard some noise, looked out the window of our house and saw about ten fraternity brothers on the street corner opposite the women's dorm. There was nothing unusual about this. Students often congregated on Church Street in small groups. At about 11:30 P.M., I looked out the window again. At this point, over fifty students were congregating on the corner and the noise level had increased substantially. I began to worry and so did Susan. What was happening?

As midnight approached the collection of students had grown and I was convinced that a full-blown insurrection was under way. I called Campus Police. "This is Roger Martin," I said calmly. "I believe a riot is taking place in front of our house." The dispatcher then said, "What is your address, please?" "This is Roger Martin," my voice rising a few octaves, since by this time there were at least two hundred students now assembled on the corner, "Please send the police immediately." "How do you spell your name?" the dispatcher persisted. "Damn it! This is the *president!!* Send the police or else!!!" Of course, once the police arrived five minutes later, the water had been dumped and everyone had disappeared, the tradition having been repeated for the sixty-sixth year.

I suppose not much can be done about the visibility problem short of wearing a T-shirt clearly marked "NEW PRESIDENT." A good sense of humor is helpful. But this particular disability is only temporary. New presidents get known quickly enough!

A second erroneous assumption new presidents often make is that the community hangs on every word they utter. This is because most of us come to the job with healthy egos. We did not get to where we are by being restrained. As vice presidents, provosts and deans, we were important and we were listened to! As new presidents, however, we tend to fall victim to what I will call "The Grand Pronouncement Syndrome," believing, in a variation of the old E. F. Hutton ad, that when the president speaks, everyone listens. It is probably true in large bureaucratic corporations that when the CEO speaks, everyone does listen. Corporate CEOs have great power because they can fire subordinates at whim. But in a college or university setting where at least half the faculty have tenure and therefore cannot arbitrarily be dismissed by the president, this is not always the case. Nor is it really the case with other members of the community.

One of my earliest grand pronouncements was made at a staff meeting in mid September. I was concerned about alcoholic beverages being illegally consumed in the football stadium during the Saturday games. It is against NCAA regulations. So, in front of my vice presidents and deans I made my first grand pronouncement. "Enough is enough. This has been going on far too long. We're going to take definitive action. At next Saturday's football game, I don't want to see any alcoholic beverages being consumed at the stadium. OK?" "OK," staff replied in unison. When Susan and I arrived at the stadium five days later, people were carting their wine coolers into the stands as usual. One of the fraternities had set up a tent on the infield and was freely dispensing beer to members and apparently anybody else who happened to be hanging around. Even the man selling tickets was quaffing a Miller Lite.

Students also have a low tolerance for presidential grand pronouncements, something that I discovered near the end of September. I had asked the dean of students to arrange a town meeting with students from a particular dorm. This would be an opportunity for me to make grand pronouncements on my vision for the college and to get student reaction. About seventy-five students appeared for this meeting, which really impressed me. Student attendance at some of the college's fall semester public lectures had been minimal. So I spoke brilliantly of the new dorms we would build, improvements we would make in the student union and so forth, and I went on like this for about forty-five minutes. I then asked if anyone had questions or comments. A glazed look appeared in almost everyone's eyes. The hour was late. And then, out of nowhere, the associate dean of students appeared with a wagonful of ice cream sundaes. I was abandoned, everyone leaping for the midnight snack. It dawned on me that maybe I was the secondary reason for the large turnout.

New presidents probably ought to suppress their desire to make grand pronouncements until they have been in office for at least a couple of months. It takes that long to get the lay of the land and in any case, premature pontifications that miss the mark will haunt you later on.

Related to the grand pronouncement syndrome is a third and final assumption new presidents often make just after they arrive on campus, namely the mistaken belief that the community is ready to accept change, even benign change, just because it is inflicted by the institution's new leader. Colleges are generally traditional and conservative places, and change happens neither quickly nor easily. But as we all know, institutions that do not keep pace with a changing society atrophy and die. Presidents exist to coax, cajole, and even bribe cautious or resisting faculty, staff, and even students to change. But change requires patience, and in very few instances can it take place in a radical way during the first month of a new president's tenure. I found this out quickly enough!

The first innovation of my presidency was more in the realm of symbolism than of substance. It was to suggest changes in the "Beginning of the Year Faculty Picnic" held late each August. In former years, the picnic had featured family games like horseshoe contests, burlap bag races, peanut hunts and the like. This year, however, I decided that the picnic would be much more informal and unorganized, a quiet occasion for me and my family to meet the families of my new colleagues. But when I arrived at the picnic, one of the emeriti faculty approached me and asked, "Aren't you going to bring back the faculty softball game?" "What faculty softball game?" I countered. "I told the faculty this would be an informal affair. No organized games!" "You ought to reconsider, President Martin. During Raymond Haupert's administration in the fifties we had a regular faculty softball game. The president always played second base and faculty participation was expected! No excuses!!" I refused to give in, but the symbolism of this tradition was not lost on me.

Being a new president is exhilarating. But it is also lonely, especially during the first few weeks. New presidents sometimes forget that a leadership change in a college or university can be a traumatic affair. Even in the best of circumstances, not everyone is excited about the arrival of a new president. My situation, I think, was typical. My predecessor served the college excellently for seventeen years. He had accomplished many important things but felt that seventeen years was enough and that the institution would benefit from new leadership. But while old presidents depart and new ones arrive, the institution itself initially seems to move along on its own momentum as though nothing ever changed.

Moravian College is 250 years old and has had over nineteen heads since its founding. Most have provided excellent leadership; some have not done as well. But despite good or bad presidents, the institution continues to exist. New presidents need to realize this. They can have a profound impact on the shape and direction of their college, but it takes time. It means initially not being recognized. It means not always being listened to in the beginning, especially when change is being suggested. It means living with the general assumption that the new president not only knows what to do, but will do it in the same way as it was done by his or her predecessors.

New presidents can ill afford to sulk over their ambiguous identities. They must quickly get on with the business of being president, and this means deciding early on how they will govern the institution. Indeed, the community, including the administration, the faculty, and the board of trustees, all wait with keen anticipation to find out whether they have inherited a despot, a benevolent dictator, a politician, or a jellyfish who can't make decisions.

I had early decided that my own style of leadership would depend on a lateral, rather than vertical, approach to decision making. My Quaker commitment to consensus decision making played a major part in causing me to adopt this style of leadership. But so did my experience at Oxford University, where I had been a graduate student. At Oxford, the faculty or fellows of a college always consult with each other before making important decisions. Consequently, while reserving the right to make all final decisions (and take responsibility for them), I saw the vice presidents and deans on the one hand and the faculty on the other as colleagues and partners in the decision-making process. I believed that decisions made by the president—which I should stress are ultimately the president's to make—should be made only after a great deal of community discussion and consultation. The vertical, authoritarian, and hierarchical mode of leadership has much to recommend it, of course. Decisions can be made quickly and decisively. But while a lateral form of leadership involving extensive discussion and consultation is more time-consuming, it better fits, in my opinion, the nature and purpose of the academy. I came to Moravian with this philosophy of leadership, based on experience and belief, and found that I was far ahead of the game, simply because I knew from the start how I wanted to lead. I made mistakes. But my leadership style had a rationale and a purpose, and this was more or less understood by my colleagues.

Establishing relationships is another priority for a new president. My first challenge in this area was to shape the president's staff. What I wanted was a staff made up of a small circle of key administrators including the various deans and vice presidents. These people would meet with me each Tuesday and participate as colleagues in all critical decisions. When it was formed, I encouraged this group to argue and disagree at staff meetings—even disagree with a position I might take. But when a decision was reached we would come out of our deliberations united in whatever action had to be taken. This required a willingness and flexibility on my part to go along with the consensus when my position on a particular issue had effectively been proven untenable or unworkable by fellow staff members. On the other hand, it also meant going against the consensus when my position hadn't been so proven and swift action was required. Creating this kind of inner circle was not without risk. It initially offended a larger group of administrators that had met under my predecessor. When I recreated this group into a Community Council, meeting only once each semester primarily for information sharing purposes, hurt feelings were not altogether assuaged. On the other hand, the eight-person president's staff ensured that different ideas would be entertained in confidence before a decision was finally made. Moreover, it protected the institution from presidential totalitarianism, the worst thing, in my opinion, that can happen in a community built on the premise that an uninhibited flow of information and ideas is a good thing.

My relationship with the faculty became the next order of business. Heretofore, the faculty had not had a direct voice in administrative decision making, especially decision making affecting the budget. True, two faculty had seats on the board of trustees. But it was made very clear to them that they represented themselves, not the faculty. True also, a representative group called the Faculty Executive Council (FEC) existed before I arrived. But it did not have official status in the college's governance structure and therefore had no recognized power. Moravian's faculty, like most faculties in the late 1970s and early 1980s, were restive. They wanted a piece of the action! In fact, what they really wanted, long before I appeared on the scene, was a *convention faculty*—that is, the right to hold faculty meetings that would not be attended by the president and his staff but would, in camera, make decisions affecting the curriculum and themselves as professors. And so, early in September, I was told by a leader of this group that faculty generally lacked confidence in the administration and wanted to meet by themselves. This person, at least, was diplomatic. Another, less artful, member of the group was more specific, stating that the faculty had long suffered without meaningful power; that promises had been made by the previous administration (a statement that turned out not to be true); that the matter was really out of my hands. The faculty was organizing, this person continued, and I'd better get the hell out of the way; if I didn't, a vote of no-confidence would be taken before the month was out.

Needless to say, I felt intimidated. The idea of a no-confidence vote before I had even unpacked my bags was extremely worrying. My journal entry for September 8 reflected this anxiety. I wrote: "Beginning to worry whether I can do the job, especially with the faculty threatening significantly to alter the College's governance." My concern was heartfelt. I had long believed that faculty should participate fully in decisions governing the curriculum, and in many noncurricular decisions as well. But I was firmly opposed to any faculty meeting in which the administration could not participate. Moreover, as the leader of the college and with ultimate responsibility for its welfare I was not about to abrogate the sacred trust given to me by the board of trustees. It looked as though a stalemate was developing and that, even before I began my term as president, I would have an unwanted showdown with the faculty. But I expressed my concerns openly with the FEC and was pleased to discover that most of them were reasonable people who had genuine concerns.

After extensive discussion and with the help of the dean of the college, a forty-year veteran the faculty respected (and whose support for me was critical my first year), a compromise was reached. The FEC would become an official committee of the faculty. They would consult with their colleagues and technically I could be present at these consultations. But all institutional decisions concerning the faculty and the curriculum would still be made at open faculty meetings subject, of course, to final presidential approval. The FEC would also hold monthly meetings with the president and the dean of the college, where faculty concerns would be discussed openly and candidly.

Finally, I thought, the issue had been resolved. But not quite. No sooner were negotiations over the structure of the FEC settled than a new issue appeared. It was now suggested by some faculty that a special committee of the board of trustees be formed to adjudicate disagreements between the faculty and the president. I opposed this suggestion on the grounds that it was an improper intrusion by the board into the internal affairs of the college. By then, however, the FEC had been meeting on a regular basis with the dean of the college and me, creating a much better atmosphere of trust. Indeed, these demands gave way to more substantive discussions of real issues—like faculty salaries!

But there were disappointments. Naively, I had hoped that the FEC might evolve into a group that could participate in the budget process. I even began sharing budget projections with its members. But the FEC was an advocacy group, and no advocacy group can play an unbiased role in budget deliberations. It would take three more years before a joint faculty-administration group known as the College Advisory on Planning and Priorities could be formed to advise me on institutional priorities. Only then would there be a better feeling that the faculty had input in an area that everyone knew really counted—the budget.

The other disappointment was more personal. I really wanted to be accepted by the faculty as an equal and to this end Susan and I held about ten dinner parties at our house the first fall so that we could get to know the entire faculty on a more personal basis. But from the very beginning, I was treated with great deference, and wherever I spoke, my utterances were often taken as ex cathedra pronouncements. On several occasions, I made a tongue-in-cheek comment that appeared at the next meeting of the FEC as an institutional concern. I once remember saying in a facetious way at faculty coffee that if my colleagues did not turn off the lights in their offices at night, they would be charged the additional electrical bill. Two days later I received complaints from several colleagues who had not been there, protesting this unreasonable requirement. Only until I had been at the college a year or two did the faculty get used to my sometimes off-the-cuff humor.

I also realized early in the game that I could never be a colleague among colleagues—an equal among equals. The president is the president, and even if he or she is liked by the faculty, barriers against intimacy unfortunately but necessarily exist. The reason is obvious. Presidents ultimately approve promotions and tenure, administer compensation, and on occasion fire or discipline members of the community. This cannot be done objectively or fairly when close friendships are involved. Indeed, new presidents who hire close friends or relatives for high administrative positions are asking for trouble. In later years I was able to develop professional (as opposed to intimate) friendships in the community and continue to value these friendships today. But I must say that I have always felt uncomfortable being set apart from the community solely because of my position as president and I am often very envious of my colleagues who are able to live more normal lives and enjoy close, often intimate friendships with members of the community.

While faculty and administrative relationships are important, equally important is the relationship between the president and the board of trustees and especially the chair of the board. To put it bluntly, a new president can endure demoralization in the administration and votes of no-confidence from the faculty. But if the president loses the board, and especially the chair of the board, the ball game is over. For my part, I would not want to coexist with a hostile faculty. But I remember the sage advice of the president of Middlebury College who once told me that "the Golden Rule" of survival for a college president is always to pay attention to the board.

Because Moravian is two institutions—a small theological seminary in addition to the college—I had two boards and therefore two chairs to deal with. I made sure to keep both of these people fully apprised of what was going on, especially when the institution faced a crisis. Of course, the board is not just the chair. At Moravian it is almost sixty other people equally distributed between the college and the seminary. I took great care, especially in the early months, to get to know as many of these people as possible. And even now, many years later, I still keep in close touch.

Board members are a very special breed of people. They are not paid for their services but, along with the president, bear responsibility for the college's well-being. In this coactive role they can become among the president's warmest supporters if the president keeps them informed and deals with them in an honest and straightforward manner. If this does not happen, the board can become the president's undoing. So too, individual members of the board can help fill the friendship-gap mentioned earlier. If the president cannot have intimate friendships with people in the immediate college community, he or she can enjoy such friendships with trustees, who are not beholden to the president for their jobs.

Unfortunately, new presidents often maintain an arm's-length relationship with members of the board, fearful that the board might meddle with presidential prerogative. They soon discover, however, that the board is made up of people with many different skills and most are just waiting to be asked by the president to lend a helping hand. The board member who is an accountant will be happy to give the new president an independent assessment of the budget. The board member who is a lawyer can give a second opinion on a tough legal problem. And almost all are available just to sit down with the president and listen. Indeed, very few want to meddle. I was lucky. Right from the beginning the chairs of the seminary and the college boards were always available to me, as were other board members. Without them, my job would have been almost impossible.

The board of trustees and the president, then, should see each other as important allies. Indeed, the relationship is a symbiotic one. On the one hand, the president has an obligation to keep the board, and especially the chair of the board, fully informed of all important issues and to involve board members, largely through the committee structure, in the affairs of the college. The board's obligation, on the other hand, is to support the new president—especially when agreed-upon changes are about to be instituted. Above all, the board must let the president be president. Presidents who unilaterally make decisions without board involvement are asking for trouble. Conversely, boards that try to manage the college themselves compromise the president's ability to lead the institution. The board, of course, has the ultimate power to fire the president if leadership is not forthcoming. But short of this final impasse, the balance between board responsibilities and presidential prerogative should be carefully maintained.

Much more could be said about getting started than I have been able to include here. New presidents must deal with a slew of crises the first year, establish a bold vision with which at least most of the community can identify, deal with an endless list of constituents and try to do all of this within the constraints of a seven-day work week. But of all these challenges, the building of relationships with staff members, with the faculty, and with the board of trustees is the new president's most important responsibility during the first several weeks. New presidents are invisible and perhaps unheeded when they arrive on campus. But by year's end, successful new presidents are not only well-known and heeded but also looked up to and respected by the entire community.

ROGER H. MARTIN *has been president of Moravian College in Bethlehem, Pennsylvania, since 1986. Before that he was executive assistant to the president at Middlebury College and then associate dean at Harvard Divinity School.*

What happens when a large, centrally administered community college reorganizes itself into a decentralized system with six new colleges? What follows is a brief history of the problems and successes of one of these colleges.

Surviving and Thriving

Sue A. Cox

The citizens of Houston, Texas, voted for the creation of the Houston Community College (HCC) in 1971, but provided no facilities and no tax base. To maximize its limited resources, the college leased space in area high schools and offered classes almost entirely in the evening. As college enrollment grew, the number of leased and borrowed facilities multiplied. A central system coordinated this assortment of centers, sending out faculty to teach wherever classes were being held. Faculty members had no home base other than their division offices, and the college did not have a very high profile in the community.

By 1990, HCC had grown to a college of over twenty-five thousand students. It had acquired a small tax base and a few facilities of its own, and was fast outgrowing its highly centralized system. The college's long-time president was retiring, setting the stage for major changes.

In 1991, the Board of Trustees hired a chancellor of the Houston Community College System (HCCS) and charged him with the responsibility of reorganizing. His response was to create six colleges that were to operate as constituent parts of the new system. He divided the college's service area into quadrants, assigning four colleges to operate as regional entities, inheriting whatever centers were already operating in those parts of the city. The colleges were named for their quadrants—Northwest, Southwest, Northeast, and Southeast. In addition he named an already existing campus in downtown Houston as the Central College and created a College Without Walls to operate as an entrepreneurial arm of the system.

I had worked at HCCS since 1973, almost from its beginning. When reorganization arrived, I was dean of social sciences, with the responsibility of operating that program across all the campuses and centers. I knew from my experience in trying to operate an ever-larger centralized system that changes were due. I applied and was named as president of the Southwest College.

Six of us were inaugurated at one time as new presidents. From the time we were approved in the spring of 1991 until HCC officially divided into colleges and we took over operations in our sectors in February 1992, we went through an arduous and intensive reorganization effort. Along with the chancellor and four new vice chancellors, we struggled to reconfigure the system. Boundaries had to be drawn; resources had to be divided; faculty and staff had to be reassigned with all the attendant difficulties that each change caused. I was committed to the new organization and was working very hard to help make it happen, but found myself torn by the loss of an organizational structure that I had been working with for years. The social sciences faculty members were moving to the new colleges. In one sense, I was losing a family.

The college culture that most people knew began to disappear before our eyes. New people were arriving with different ideas about how to do things and did not seem too impressed with what we had accomplished over the years. Suddenly, many of us felt the urge to defend what we had done and to point out the heroic efforts that had been involved in keeping HCCS going in the lean years. I personally worried that my own long experience at HCCS might not be diverse enough to measure up to the backgrounds of the new people. While the presidents and vice chancellors grew closer together as they tried to reorganize, many others felt left out of the process and isolated from the major alterations that were taking place. Jobs were changing and everyone worried about where they would land. We were in the throes of culture shock.

In fact, the actual period of reorganization was probably the time the executive group was the most cohesive. It felt as we were all in a lifeboat in rough seas. If anyone rocked the boat too hard we would all capsize. This feeling, however, did not last long. We got ourselves organized and took up very different kinds of roles. The presidents had to make their colleges flourish and the vice chancellors had to think of what was best for the system as a whole. Natural conflicts began to emerge.

Each of the regional colleges represented a different sector of the metropolitan area with its own constituency. The college presidents represented those needs at the system level, competing for the limited resources that the system could provide. We inherited whatever facilities and programs were already in our region, and these varied widely from college to college. We worked together to improve programs systemwide, but we also sought to protect and expand the assets in our colleges.

In reality, the regional advocacy that we naturally began to bring to the table was a positive change. Needs from all over the metropolitan area began to be enunciated and represented in system deliberations. The key to the balance between destructive competition for resources and healthy advocacy was the quality of the planning that the system fostered and the ability of each college, when necessary, to think beyond its own district's needs to what could benefit the whole system. Each college, in turn, had to receive some degree of attention and help from the system. The parallels to district-elected representatives were obvious. The system functioned well as long as we tended our constituents' needs but didn't forget our responsibilities to the health of the whole. We had both successes and failures in this area.

The new Southwest College covered a huge territory from close to the downtown area to the western suburbs. Although HCCS boundaries were created to be congruent with the Houston Independent School District boundaries, the Southwest College also served one out-of-district area with its own school district, as well as the town of Stafford, which had voted to be annexed into HCCS. We had, to put it politely, a potpourri of what we euphemistically called campuses. We offered evening classes in eight high schools and three middle schools, sharing facilities with the public schools. We leased the top floor of an office building in an excellent business location near downtown, and owned two other facilities. The Gulfton Center was a small office building that the college had bought to house an intensive English program. Part of the second floor of this building became our administrative offices. It was the only place in the college that had any space that could house us.

We also owned about five acres of land with two converted warehouses in Stafford. Apart from the Central College, these two buildings housed the system's largest campus. By running classes seven days and nights a week, we enrolled over four thousand students at the Stafford Campus. Combining all our facilities and programs in the Southwest area, our reorganized administration found itself with over twelve thousand students, taking everything from flower arranging to air conditioning technology to physics.

There was good news and bad news for our new college. We had an excellent group of faculty members. Most were happy to be in the Southwest College and all were used to the rigors of teaching in borrowed facilities and converted office buildings. We had a strong academic program and a few major technical programs such as data processing and technical communication. The Intensive English program was considered one of the best in the area and was growing rapidly.

In many cases, however, the pieces that made up the college were just that—pieces. Because everything had been run out of a centralized administration, we had several technical programs that were part-time outposts of the larger program located somewhere else. Some of these we continued to operate in conjunction with the college that had the primary center of the program, but others were inferior versions that were clearly rusting in the backwater. One of our tasks was to choose those programs that we felt could be helped to stand alone and become high-quality offerings. We gave primary attention to three of these piecemeal programs—office occupations, air conditioning technology, and drafting technology. With dedicated full-time staff, an influx of new equipment, and advisory committees, two of the three programs (office occupations and air conditioning technology) took off, with enrollments growing very quickly.

We also had to decide what new technical programs we could begin with the limited space we had available. We began an industrial electricity program—first as an extension of the air conditioning program and then, with the strong support of an advisory committee, as a stand-alone program, still sharing some space but operating independently.

We had to be careful with the number of new programs we undertook as our resources and space were severely limited. First we sought to improve what we already had and then create related programs that could share space and attain independence gradually.

Of all the new colleges in the system, we were most dependent on shared high school facilities. We took over in the evening, working with the high schools to use their classrooms and labs. We had all the difficulties that inevitably arise when two groups are using the same facilities. There were, to be sure, small irritations, but the larger problems revolved around how to offer the kinds of programs that students increasingly needed when we did not have major access to the facilities. If we bought computers for the labs, we only got to use them in the evenings. High school science labs were inadequate, and if we tried to upgrade them, we were faced with storage and security problems. When we had to make choices about how to use the limited funds we had to upgrade equipment, we inevitably chose to put it in the places that we had access to all the time. The result was that our students who attended the high schools were increasingly cut out of the most up-to-date programs. Further, as the demand increased for day classes, we had to assign more of our full-time faculty to those classes. The result was that our evening facilities depended largely on part-time faculty and staff.

The Southwest College was also heavily tied to shared evening facilities at a time when Houston citizens, like citizens from big cities all over the country, began to view the night as a dangerous time. They were more cautious about going out, and they also began to think carefully about where they were willing to go. Many of the high school campuses were not viewed as being secure. Parking was usually inadequate or remote from classes, and parking lots were poorly lighted. While the tax-paying citizens of Houston loved the idea of having the colleges share facilities with high schools, they increasingly turned away from them as students. Instead, they opted for the more comprehensive facilities that offered up-to-date equipment, complete programs, and a college atmosphere. The result was that the few day-night facilities we had were growing while the high school centers were declining in enrollment. Since two-thirds of our enrollment was dependent on evening classes in the high schools, we began to show an overall decline in enrollment.

Declines in enrollment were also accelerated by the rapidly changing demographics in much of southwest Houston. We had been operating in some of the high schools since 1971, when the areas surrounding them were suburban neighborhoods. Over the intervening years, the city had surrounded these areas, and what had once been outlying areas were now busy and diverse parts of the inner city. We needed to expand our programs to meet the 1995 needs of southwest Houston. The high school facilities gave us very little flexibility for that.

The assumption from the beginning of reorganization was that the HCCS would go to the citizens with a bond issue, providing the funds to create comprehensive campuses in the regional colleges. Most of the planning and hopes for the new organization revolved around this assumption. In November 1993, HCCS did go out for a $300 million bond issue, and Houston answered with a resounding "no."

A number of things went wrong, but the biggest problem was that we had almost no community-based identity. We were still an ephemeral presence that, for the most part, was viewed as the folks who turned the lights on at night in the high schools, stayed awhile, and left. The colleges had been in existence for less than two years and were only beginning to realize the enormous need for a greater community presence and the kind of base that most community colleges take for granted. The city's largest newspaper editorialized that the HCCS was doing very well in its borrowed facilities and that they should not seek a "Cadillac" when a "Chevrolet" would do ("Reject HCCS Bonds," 1993). Robert Reich's touting of the community college as a major hope for technical training had not had much effect yet, and the idea of shared facilities seemed compelling to taxpayers who did not really know much about what HCCS did or what plans it had for its future.

The failure of the bond issue left the Southwest College in desperate need of adequate space for expansion, where we could begin to build state-of-the-art programs that would educate and train people in our part of the city. There was no HCCS money available for building in the Southwest part of the city and very little prospect of any.

Fortunately, the Southwest College had an impressive and ardent supporter in the city of Stafford. By 1994, Leonard Scarcella had been mayor of Stafford for over twenty years. He began his tenure the year after he graduated from law school and continued uninterrupted to lead this town of approximately ten thousand. He was an eloquent supporter of the HCCS and the Southwest College, as was the city council and most of the town's citizens. The Stafford experience was, in fact, the ideal interaction of community college and community. It was, in microcosm, what we hoped could happen in the many communities that make up Houston.

But Stafford is not an isolated small town. It sits on the crossroads of West Houston. Students from all over the southwest part of the city attend the campus. There was clearly a demand to be met and a chance to grow in this community. Moreover, land was available adjacent to our converted warehouse campus. The question was how to find the funds to buy the land and create a new facility.

Mayor Scarcella provided our answer. He offered to explore the possibility that perhaps there was some way that the city of Stafford might help the college by providing funds through a city bond issue for the first building of what could eventually become a comprehensive campus. Working with HCCS, Scarcella began leading the effort to create a precedent-setting partnership between a community and a college. Essentially what was being proposed was a $7.5 million bond issue to buy land and construct a building. HCCS would then lease the land and facility from Stafford. The annual rent payments would equal or exceed the debt service. When the bonds were paid off, the building and land would be transferred to HCCS. Additional land would be bought by HCCS to create a sufficient base for the future planning of a comprehensive campus.

Stafford and HCCS maintained that the legal basis for such a partnership was Article 3, Section 52a of the Texas Constitution and the related Article 835s of the Texas Civil Statutes. We argued that these provisions are applicable to "developing and diversifying the economy and eliminating unemployment or underemployment in the state" (Scarcella and Cox, 1994, p. 1). We made the argument that community colleges are intricately involved in the future economic well-being of the communities they served and that the partnership we were proposing would aid in this process.

While there were a number of legal hurdles to be overcome, the most exciting set of events for me was the effort on the part of the college to convince the people of Stafford that they should vote for a new partnership between themselves and HCCS. Since we had been in Stafford for a number of years, we felt we had a good reputation for quality programs. With the advice of Scarcella and the help of many people both in and out of the college, we embarked on a local campaign to get a yes vote on election day. With the volunteer efforts of students, faculty, staff, and community members, we created a committee that we entitled the Stafford Political Action Committee for Expansion (SPACE). It was a campaign done in miniature, following all the legal requirements, and it energized the college. We did not have many of the problems faced by HCCS in the Houston bond issue election. We had a specific project to talk about, we were part of the community, and we had a small electorate. We could almost directly reach every resident of Stafford. Some real leaders among the staff emerged to lead the political effort. My role was to make our case to the city. I made presentations to the City Council and to a Stafford town meeting, telling them about our need and also what we thought we could do that would benefit them.

For me, there was a pivotal moment that brought everything that was good about the campaign into sharp focus. About a dozen of us stood outside the Stafford city hall on election night and waited for the results. It was a chilly January evening but we stayed close to the front door, waiting and talking. We were administrators, students, faculty, and Stafford citizens. Officials inside posted a hand-written notice of results on the inside of the glass door, and we crowded around to see. We had won with 241 for and 19 votes against. The margin might as well have been a million. We celebrated with the joy of having been totally and successfully committed to something and the camaraderie of mutual effort.

If all goes well, the Southwest College should have a new facility by fall 1996. It will house major new technical programs as well as new general classroom space. It will provide the base from which the adjunct programs at our night campuses can draw strength and resources. It is the beginning of a major community college base for the college and for the area.

Looking back on the brief history of the Southwest College, my single defining experience as a new president has been a seemingly unending search for space—day space, modern space, space with adequate parking, safe space, available space, space for high technology. I have been in dozens of office buildings, vacant warehouses, and closed convenience stores. I have talked to real estate developers, agents, building owners, and land speculators. Four years ago, I had no idea how big a thousand square feet was. Now I know what it will hold and how to calculate it by counting ceiling tiles. I know what temporary buildings cost and I know how long it takes to put them up. In a speech recently, when asked what my vision for the Southwest College was, I replied that I had a dream in which the letters PPL flashed repeatedly before my eyes. I awoke to the revelation that my vision was a Perfect Parking Lot. To put it mildly, this is not how I thought I would be spending much of my time as a college leader.

Late on summer Saturday afternoons, I get out the lawn mower and mow my front yard. I go up and down in straight rows and every so often I stop and look behind me with a sense of satisfaction. I can see right before my eyes what I have accomplished. The grass is neatly in place. I have made a difference and it was for the best. What a relief to have an activity in which the decisions are easy and the results are always positive. While the neatness of the grass-cutting process is not enough to make me change my career to yards and shrubs, it does make me yearn for the hands-on ability to make immediate changes. Everything takes longer than I thought it would, and almost every direct intervention in ongoing processes causes complications I didn't expect.

After I sweat through a Houston afternoon mowing my lawn, I sit in the shade and proudly observe the job I have done. Asking pardon for the homespun philosophy, it occurs to me that the quality of my neighborhood is, at least in small part, dependent on the job I do in taking care of my property. I am persuaded to do the work because if I didn't, I wouldn't be meeting the expectations of my neighborhood. A community college lives very much within the needs and expectations of a much-expanded neighborhood. As a college leader, I can do good work as I help to understand and interpret community needs and as I link the college with the community at large. I can also help the college develop its own cohesive community. When we were a centralized entity, we were so big that each area had its turf and defended it. If things did not go right, instruction blamed counseling, counseling had difficulties with campus administration, and so on. The most difficult and important job is to lead in the creation of a college community in which everyone has a stake in all the parts needed to provide outstanding instruction to students.

Frequently on my way downtown, I take the route that goes by Rice University. As I drive under the shade of the huge live oaks that border the campus, I catch glimpses of manicured lawns and stately buildings, beautifully serene and protected from the rush of traffic on the street. While I enjoy the view and recognize the quality of what I see, I know that our converted warehouses and rented facilities serve an equally important purpose in Houston. We do our work in the chaos and excitement of the city, without the academy environment but with an understanding of our students' needs and with a desire to be part of the educational answer to the problems and possibilities that are part of the future of this country.

References

"Reject HCCS Bonds." *Houston Chronicle,* Oct. 19, 1993, p. 10B. Editorial.

Scarcella, L., and Cox, S. A. *Economic Benefits of Proposed Improvement to the Houston Community College System Stafford Campus.* Unpublished manuscript, 1994.

SUE A. COX *is president of Southwest College in Houston, Texas.*

A new president encounters a controversy over the name of his university's athletic teams and must decide how to approach this issue.

Confronting Value Conflicts

Paul G. Risser

Miami University, chartered in 1809, opened its doors with twenty-four students in 1824. Its beautiful residential campus is located in southwestern Ohio, in the valley of the Little Miami and Great Miami Rivers. These rivers were named for the native Miami Indians, who lived in the region from 1700 until most of the tribe was forcefully removed to Kansas in 1840 and then to Oklahoma in 1867. It is from this region and for these people that Miami University is named. Today, Miami is a selective, liberal education, doctoral university with twenty thousand students on three campuses.

Upon arriving as Miami's nineteenth president on January 1, 1993, almost immediately I encountered the continuing and frequently heated topic concerning the name of our athletic teams, the Miami Redskins. To many people, the term is considered racist or at least highly insensitive; to others, it is a name reflecting great pride in the region and in the native peoples for whom the University is named.

For most of Miami's first hundred years, the nickname was not an issue as the teams were referred to as simply Miami, Big Red, or similar names. In 1916, the athletic teams were described as the Big Red Team, but the college yearbook, *Recensio*, was designed with an Indian motif and key seniors were identified as "Big Chiefs." The yearbook contained the "Scalp Song," coauthored by Alfred Upham, who later became the fourteenth President of the University. In the intervening years, there were no Indian motifs in the yearbook until the 1923 version, when pictures of Indian sculptures appeared. In 1927, the term Tribe Miami was first used, there were pictures of students dressed as Indians, and the athletic lettermen were described as "Tribe Miami."

In 1931, the term Redskin appeared in the *Recensio*. In 1932, the Redskin logo appeared, first on cheerleaders' uniforms and then on various campus images. The 1936 *Alumni News* states that "Miami reveled in the name 'Big

Reds' until 1928 when R.J. McGuiness, Miami publicity director, coined the term 'Redskins.'" Thus, the term Redskin has an informal origin, and it began when the University was approximately 120 years old.

From about 1930 until the early 1970s, the use of the term Redskin and several related symbols spread in many directions, including a mascot called Hia-wa-bop, a costumed warrior, from the 1950s to 1972. In 1972, the University's seventeenth President, Phillip R. Shriver, appointed a task force to examine the use of the name Redskin and associated issues. As a result of these deliberations, use of the term Redskin was reaffirmed, though Hia-wa-bop was abolished as the mascot, to be replaced by Chief Miami; this individual was to be trained in dance by the Miami Tribe and to be costumed in authentic fancy dancer regalia. The University also adopted a policy eliminating all derogatory caricatures of Indians and stated that "all dress and activities depicting Indians at athletic events or wherever Indian symbols are used must be authentic, dignified, and in good taste."

Miami University has a unique and very close relationship with the federally recognized Miami Tribe of Oklahoma, from which it received its name. This relationship is an unusually sincere and personal one. The university takes great pride in the tribe, and current and past students speak in very caring ways about the tribe. The tribe considers Miami to be "their university," the chief and other members of the tribe frequently visit the university, and a few young people from the tribe attend Miami. The university and the tribe mutually treasure and respect this strong relationship and continually seek to enhance their partnership.

Background: Early Spring 1993

Early in the spring semester of 1993, shortly after my arrival, the University Senate passed a resolution stating that the term Redskin would no longer be used as the nickname of the university's athletic teams. Under university procedures, such resolutions are forwarded to the board of trustees through the president, who may choose to offer a recommendation. At about this time, the student newspaper, *The Miami Student,* decided and stated that it would no longer use the term Redskin in its publication.

Several circumstances triggered these events. Mascot names were being debated at several colleges, and there was ongoing national discussion about the Washington Redskins, the Atlanta Braves, and the Cleveland Indians. At Miami, a number of student leaders, including the president of the Associated Student Government, took up the challenge of forcing the University to abandon the name Miami Redskins. In addition, as a new president who arrived from New Mexico and was a native of Oklahoma, it was felt by many that, from this close association with Native Americans, I would be more receptive to a change in the name of the mascot.

Deciding Whether or Not to Engage the Issue. At this point, there were several options that I considered as president. In brief, the options were to transmit the senate resolution to the board without any recommendations, make a unilateral decision either to retain or eliminate the nickname, engage in thorough discussion before making a decision, or ignore the issue in any formal manner and let the various points of view be argued in spontaneous forums.

The simplest decision would have been to pass along the senate's resolution to the board of trustees without any recommendation. Although the outcome is uncertain, after heated discussion at one or more board meetings, it is very likely that the board would have voted to retain the name. Adopting this option would have shielded the president from much of the pressure—the constituent groups would have aimed their most intensive lobbying and arguments at the board, whose members would have made the final decision.

If the president had made a unilateral decision to retain the Redskin name, it is likely that the board would have upheld the decision; if the president had decided to change the name, the board would probably not have upheld the decision. In either case, the losing side would have argued vehemently that its position was not heard and that it was treated unfairly. Moreover, the losing side would probably not have changed its practices. That is, if the decision had been to eliminate the term Redskin from use, it would have continued to appear clandestinely, as has happened at other institutions when unilateral decisions have been made. A more interesting political option, of course, would have been for the president to have decided to eliminate the name Redskin and then to have the board overturn this decision. In this instance, the president would have satisfied those who wanted to eliminate the term, and the board would have satisfied those who wished to retain it.

As president, I could have (at least) attempted to ignore or delay the issue and not have brought forth the senate's recommendation. After making the legitimate argument that its wishes were being stonewalled, the senate would have requested an audience with the board, and it is likely that spontaneous demonstrations of various types would have arisen. If the senate had not raised the issue, it would have been raised by other constituencies on campus, and the options would have been the same, with proposals being presented directly to the board of trustees.

All three of these options would have left the board in the position of making a decision without the strong leadership of the president.

From the outset, it was abundantly clear that this was an intense no-win situation. There were very strong and deep feelings on both sides, and both sides could not be simultaneously satisfied. In many ways, however, this issue is no different from others facing our society, such as abortion, gun control, welfare entitlement programs, or even foreign aid. Very reasonable people, with strong moral and ethical values, come to very different decisions.

After considering the alternatives, and asking myself if there were ways in which the situation could become part of an enriched learning experience, it was clear that the university should engage the issue. In so doing, Miami University had an opportunity to make a significant contribution to the resolution of issues such as these.

To be successful in developing a model for these complicated discussions and decisions, our process needed to provide an environment that encouraged open sharing of ideas and a respect for different points of view. Simply voting on the issue was not the point, since this would not have involved additional learning. There should be an abundance of informed discussion—discussion in which the participants take the time and make the effort to study the issue, not simply leap to an initial position and defend that position at all costs.

Decision Process. Miami used a thorough process for considering the use of the term Redskin, involving many constituencies and venues. A detailed package of information was placed on reserve in all the libraries, many discussion groups and sessions were organized, and the topic was discussed in several classes and in both student and commercial newspapers. Alumni chapters were sent information and urged to discuss the topic, as was the athletic booster club. The most widely advertised and attended event was a forum held in the field house in which approximately 120 speakers spoke for up to three minutes each. As president, I moderated the entire forum, recognizing each speaker, making notes as appropriate, and expressing appreciation for every statement. The forum was orderly, with different groups expressing support for statements with which they agreed and little or no disparagement of opposing views. All those who requested the opportunity to speak did so and, perhaps by chance, were evenly split between those who spoke for changing and those who spoke for retaining the name. A special session was held for the board of trustees, where its members heard presentations on both sides of the issue from representative students, staff, faculty, and alumni. In addition, persons were encouraged to write to the president and offer opinions and advice.

After all this consideration, there were those who sincerely believed that the name should be changed and those who thought it should be retained. Those who believed it should be changed argued one or more of the following points: that the name is derogatory, racist, and insensitive; that it conveys the wrong image of Native Americans; that nicknames of athletic teams can be changed without harming the long-term identity of the institution; and that a university, as a place where all people and ideas should be respected, should have no nicknames which denote otherwise. Those who believed in maintaining the status quo argued that the name was initially selected to honor the American Indians; that it is not meant to be negative and that it connotes positive characteristics; that it has developed a strong and respectful tradition; that their use of the term does not mean disrespect and therefore the term cannot be disrespectful; and that the move to change it comes largely from a few people who are concerned about what is currently termed a "politically correct" point of view.

Several other universities and colleges also have considered changes in nicknames or symbols that denote Native Americans. In some cases, there has been change and in others the status quo has been maintained. In virtually every one of these cases, regardless of the ultimate decision, the issue has remained divisive, in some cases for years and even decades. This is not surprising, especially when decisions have been made without inclusive and comprehensive consideration. Continuing conflict over the issue occurs because there is no answer that satisfies all parties, nor is there an objective method for deciding what all persons should think or believe.

Role of the Miami Tribe. As recently as 1990, the Miami Tribe was asked for its opinion on the name Redskin, and it stated that it was agreeable to the continued use of the term. This was an important statement because many of those in this discussion argued that it should be left to the tribe to decide. That is, if the tribe had no disagreement with the continued use of the term, then it should be continued. In this more recent discussion in 1993, the tribe chose not to participate directly. As one would expect among any group of people, there were members of the tribe who believed the name should be changed, others thought it should be retained, and many had no particular opinion or believed the issue to be unimportant. The tribe, however, supported the process by which the issue was being considered and said it would support the decision made by the president.

Early in the process, the tribe indicated that if a change in the nickname were made, the tribe would ask that the symbolism between the university and the tribe persist and that any other nickname continue to convey the strong relationship between the university and the tribe. If no change were made in the name, the tribe would ask that the name Redskin continue to be used with the utmost care and respect.

Institutional Values and the Decision

The nickname is not the fundamental issue in itself—it is a manifestation of personal beliefs and of institutional values. There is a very serious question about the degree to which an institution should attempt to dictate the beliefs and statements of its members and constituents. An academic institution by its very nature is committed to free inquiry and to promoting a search for knowledge. While recognizing the dignity of individual members of the community, an academic institution is not and should not be engaged in promoting a particular ideology or denying individuals the right to hold unpopular positions. Fundamental to the process of learning is the ability of an individual to question the conventional wisdom, to refine the teachings being offered, and to derive his or her own values.

At Miami University, it is our fundamental position that individuals should become as informed as possible on issues in question, should recognize their individual responsibility to society as a whole as well as to themselves, and should develop a set of values on which to make judgments and base decisions. The role of the university is to provide an environment which supports this personal intellectual development, including the ability to make decisions and to anticipate and accept the consequences of those decisions.

Decision. Miami University retains as one of its hallmarks an intellectual environment that encourages respectful and informed debate. Indeed, a major purpose of this university is to assist students as they clarify their values and reach responsible decisions. In this environment, all the participants, be they students, faculty, staff, parents, alumni, or community members, are expected as individuals to form views and beliefs based on thoughtful analysis and sound moral judgments. Thus, in my opinion, each person should be called upon to decide whether he or she wishes to use the term Redskin. This individual decision should be based on careful and informed thought, the values of the person, and his or her responsibilities to others and to society.

Miami University also has values and responsibilities. One of its responsibilities is to value its people and to ensure that these persons can grow intellectually in a reasoned, fair, and respectful environment. Appellations help create this environment. To many, the nickname Redskin implies a disrespectful environment. Conversely, to others, the nickname does not imply any disrespect. Therefore, as an institution that encourages independent thought, as president, I decided that the institutional use of the term Redskin as a nickname for the university's athletic teams would be addressed in the following way:

- Only those university athletic organizations and athletic publications currently using the nickname Redskin may continue to use the nickname. Whenever the term Redskin is used, the name and any symbol of peoples and cultures must continue to be represented authentically, with dignity and respect. The use of the nickname Redskin shall not be expanded beyond representations where it currently appears.

- All other organizations sponsored by the university and official publications of the university not covered above will use the term Miami Tribe as the nickname of the athletic teams. The word tribe is defined by Webster in part as "A group of persons, families, or clans believed to be descended from a common ancestor and forming a close community." This clearly describes the unique relationship between Miami University and the Miami Tribe of Oklahoma, and it responds to the tribe's request that the name retain the symbolism between the tribe and the university. The nickname Miami Tribe provides an alternative for those who believe that the term Redskin does not convey the sensitive environment that must exist at Miami University. The university's linkage with a proud Native American people, even in the very name of the institution, can be preserved with dignity indefinitely through the use of the words Miami Tribe.

Discussion. It would have been relatively easy for me to have made a simple decision either to discard or retain the Redskin name, but neither of these outcomes, although they would have engendered approval from some quarters, would have been the right decision. Had that happened, one part of the community would have won and another part would have lost. There would have been continued discussion because the university would have attempted to dictate beliefs to individuals, to state what is right or wrong, when in fact the answer must come from individual values and judgments. Far more significantly, each of us would suddenly have been absolved of thinking about the implications of this issue any further. By providing an alternative, the university does not divide the community. More important, as a result of this recommendation, each of us as a person, as members of campus athletic organizations, or through involvement with athletic publications was required to continue to examine our values and responsibilities, decide how we use words, and reflect on how our thoughts and ideas affect and are affected by other people and cultures.

The process of considering this issue was extremely important as a model for discussing complex topics, and the university involved its broad community in resolving it. Acceptance of the nickname Redskin has been reasserted when individuals, athletic organizations, and those involved with athletic publications have carefully considered the implications as brought forth during the deliberative process. Alternatively, the term Tribe may be used by those who prefer it; its use is also supported by the Miami Tribe of Oklahoma. As part of the recommendation, I established a task force to make recommendations to strengthen the relationship between the tribe and the university. Most of the task force recommendations have now been implemented.

Action of the Board of Trustees. After considerable discussion at the designated meeting, the board of trustees voted to accept the president's recommendation. The vote was four positive, three negative, one abstention, and one absentee positive vote, which was not officially counted. This very close vote reflected the continued division of opinion on the issue, even after exhaustive and extended discussion.

My recommendation was a surprise to virtually all in the community; it had been widely expected that the answer would be either to continue or discontinue the name. The initial reaction was that the decision was either no decision at all or that it was a reasonable compromise. Over time, others have come forth to applaud the recommendation, and if a poll were taken today, there would be a significant number of people in all of these camps.

During the past year and a half, the issue of the nickname has arisen only occasionally on campus and throughout the broader community. The term Tribe is rarely used, and Redskin or simply Miami are the predominant terms used for the university's athletic teams.

Concluding Thoughts

Discussion of the Redskin issue consumed a large amount of time and energy. Thus, a reasonable question is whether or not it was worth all the effort and, if we were to do it again, whether or not the issue should have been raised. Of course, there is no experimental control; that is, one cannot predict the situation today had we not decided to engage the issue.

On the negative side, much time and energy were devoted to this issue, and, thus, there may have been opportunity costs in terms of what could have been accomplished otherwise. Questions were raised as to whether the new president understood the tradition of the Redskins and whether such an issue should be raised so early in his term, or even if the issue should ever be raised.

And, there was some polarization on the campus, although without exception, this resulted in very civilized exchanges. Many of those most strongly interested in encouraging diversity on campus were disappointed that the name was not changed, thereby sending a strong message that diversity was welcomed and encouraged. It should be noted, however, that there were ethnic minorities on both sides of the issue.

On the positive side, the campus and the community were able to discuss a very volatile issue in great depth and with strong passion but to do so in a civilized manner. In addition, this process led by the president signaled that the campus would be open to serious debate, but that such discussion should be based on information and judgments rather than on emotion and previously held views. There are no quantitative data, but it appeared that a small number of participants changed their opinions, especially in the direction of deciding that the term Redskin might not be appropriate at this time although it might have been acceptable at other times. Virtually everyone completed the process with a better understanding of the opposing opinion. The final decision permitted (indeed, forced) individuals to reexamine their own values and to think hard about their interactions with other peoples and cultures. Those who continued to believe the term Redskin was acceptable could continue to use it, and those who thought it unacceptable had an alternative that met the expectations of the Miami Tribe.

So, on balance, if I were able to make the decision again, would we engage the issue? The answer is yes, but with even greater reluctance. Yes, because it is so important for universities, especially good ones, to provide opportunities for their members to engage in complicated issues and in so doing to learn from each other. This issue, and all its implications, is as important as any other for our students and for society at large. My reluctance arises from the great opportunity cost; that is, other important issues were neglected just because the Redskin issue required a disproportionate amount of time. Also, this issue was so dominant that it has taken much longer for me to set forth my own agenda for the university. However, had we not engaged the issue, we would still be dealing with it in smaller components, but it is unlikely that the total amount of time would have been as extensive.

PAUL G. RISSER *is president of Oregon State University in Corvallis, Oregon. He was previously president of Miami University in Oxford, Ohio.*

Today's college presidents are often faulted for not speaking out on important public policy issues as their predecessors did in years past, yet the circumstances surrounding contemporary presidents make it difficult for them to take personal stands.

Assuming the Bully Pulpit

Rita Bornstein

In the early years of my presidency, one of the most vexing issues I confronted was whether to become involved in public policy issues and political campaigns. I was urged to join an anti-casino-gambling coalition, support the political campaigns of a college alumnus and a professor, and to lobby on behalf of a local congressional representative who was seeking one of his party's key leadership roles in Congress. Seeking guidance from my more seasoned colleagues, I elicited a range of advice, from the bold, "Be outspoken; your involvement will heighten the visibility of the College," to the timid, "Be cautious, high visibility on controversial matters can threaten the good reputation of your institution." A review of the literature on the presidency turned up scant discussion of the public role of the president apart from traditional institutional activities. As my presidency evolved, it became clear to me that while the public expects presidents to provide leadership on important issues, presidents are constrained by their positions from speaking freely as independent citizens.

The prestige of the college presidency assures an audience for a president's ideas, providing a bully pulpit unequaled in most realms of public life. Despite this privileged access to the public, today's college and university presidents are perceived as silent and lacking in leadership on important public policy and political issues. There is a nostalgia for the highly visible presidents of yesteryear whose influential voices found eager audiences through national magazines, radio programs, and lecture halls around the country.

A version of this chapter called "Back in the Spotlight: The College President as Public Intellectual" was published in *Educational Record*, Fall 1995. © 1995 American Council on Education.

"A generation ago . . . college and university presidents cut striking figures on the public stage," proclaims the *New York Times*. "They called for the reform of American education, proposed safeguards for democracy, sought to defuse the cold war, urged moral standards for scientific research, and addressed other important issues of the time. Today, almost no college or university president has spoken out significantly about Bosnia, Haiti, North Korea, health care, welfare reform, the attack on the National Endowment for the Arts, or dozens of other issues high on the national agenda" (Honan, 1994).

Indeed, it is the rare president who has the time, expertise, and independence to establish a leadership role in national affairs. The college presidency is complex in scope and administrative responsibility and circumscribed by the pressures of multiple, fractious constituencies. When presidents do speak out, their voices often are lost in the cacophony of opinions, informed and uninformed, that swirl around public issues. The democratization of opinion through radio and television talk shows, call-in programs, letters to the editor, and op-ed pieces has replaced the old hierarchy of voices with educated and experienced opinion leaders at its summit. Media attention is more often captured by the mean-spirited, aggressive, and adversarial voice than by the thoughtful intellectual analyst.

Despite the strictures on their ability to speak and be heard, however, college and university presidents have an important role to play in public debate on policy issues. As Bender (1993) asserts, applying intellectual resources to civic life is a responsibility of citizenship in a democracy. On national and local issues, presidents can help raise the level of discourse above factional loyalties, contribute a broad historical perspective, identify ethical problems, provide acceptable alternatives for consideration, and stake out a position.

I presented a paper on this topic as part of a panel at a national association meeting of presidents. The reaction was so spirited that I decided to determine more systematically how today's university and college presidents define their public role, and whether they consider speaking out on public policy issues a vital part of their position and feel free to do so.

Presidents Define Their Public Role

In the summer of 1994, I conducted a survey of 230 college and university presidents about their role in public policy issues and partisan politics. The institutions surveyed are independent, coeducational, and both denominational and nondenominational. One hundred sixty-seven (73 percent) of the presidents responded, and many commented that they welcomed the opportunity to consider the issue. Of the respondents, 18 were from research universities, 70 from comprehensive institutions, and 79 from liberal arts colleges. The survey did not ask presidents about their public role on education issues because speaking, writing, and lobbying in this arena are already acknowledged as appropriate and necessary.

Most presidents reported that they do not become involved in controversial public policy issues or partisan politics, although they have strong opinions on these matters. The most frequently cited reasons were concern about offending diverse constituencies, impact on fundraising, reaction of trustees, time spent on administrative duties, and inability to stay informed on issues.

Presidents are constrained from speaking freely by their identification with the institutions they represent. Eighty-two percent of the respondents say that presidents should subordinate their personal views and political beliefs to the interests of their institutions. When a president speaks, the institution is presumed to speak: "As a private individual my viewpoints would get little public attention, but, because I am president, my public positions could easily put me on the front page of the local paper."

For many, the dissonance between personal passion and public restraint creates serious inner conflict: "While part of me wants to think that we do not have to subsume our rights as public citizens, my professional side is clearly saying that once you are a public figure you have to think in terms of the institutional and greater good before your own personal needs."

When asked if there are controversial noneducation issues on which they have a position but refrain from entering the public debate, 74 percent of the respondents said yes. Abortion, health care, sexual preference issues, the environment, and gun control were cited most frequently as examples.

However, those presidents who do take public positions on controversial noneducation issues tackle both these issues and others such as race and gender, foreign policy, and taxation. Many other issues in which presidents are involved are more local—affordable housing, crime, economic development, and public transportation, for example. Leon Botstein, the highly visible president of Bard College, commented, "A college president has an obligation to be more outspoken than the average citizen. . . . Failure to be in a leadership role on matters of public policy . . . is an act of cowardice and an avoidance of responsibility. We need to teach our students that the civilized assertion of one's beliefs is an obligation, an honor, and a pleasure."

When asked about partisan politics, 74 percent responded that presidents should not be involved. Only 19 percent endorse candidates publicly. Ten percent host fundraising events for candidates, although 37 percent of the presidents attend them. Presidents involved in partisan politics reported that they have found themselves in difficult situations, such as supporting a losing candidate or finding two long-time friends of the institution in the same race.

Despite their lack of direct involvement in partisan politics, a majority of the presidents, 55 percent, contribute to political campaigns. Several presidents indicate that their contributions are always below the amount reportable to the public.

A minority of respondents, often those who were involved in politics before they assumed the presidency, hold an activist view: "You can't avoid getting involved in politics. When the board chair gets nervous, I say that I never took an oath to give up being a citizen. I want to have a life."

Although this survey was conducted solely among independent institution presidents, the issues are familiar to presidents of public institutions as well. For example, Peter Flawn (1990, p. 184), former president of the University of Texas, Austin, advises, "The president of a public university should not be politically active and certainly should not be closely identified with a political party or movement. You should be identified as independent and bipartisan, and you should maintain friendly and cordial relations with politicians of all parties. If you have strong conservative or liberal beliefs, conceal them. . . . You must seek the image of a strong advocate for higher education who is above partisan politics and working only for the best interests of the state and the university."

The precarious balance between the president's role as institutional "logo" (McLaughlin and Riesman, 1983, p. 185) and the responsibilities of citizenship is rarely discussed among presidents, at higher education conferences, or in the literature about higher education or the public intellectual. Yet the high level of interest generated by the survey suggests that the subject requires research and deliberation.

A Different Kind of Presidency

Robert Hutchins, president of the University of Chicago for twenty-one years, and a great public intellectual, reminds us that the majority of presidents throughout history have labored in obscurity, remembered by their constituents, but never a factor on the national scene. He attacked university presidents, who, he said, "limit their utterances to platitudes. Timidity thus engendered turns into habit. . . . 'Getting on' is the great American aspiration. The way to get on is to be safe, to be sound, to be agreeable, to be inoffensive, to have no views on important matters not sanctioned by the majority, by your superiors, or by your group" (Mayer, 1993, p. 4).

A number of the college presidents I surveyed agreed that as a group they are conspicuously timid: "Higher education, at the moment, is one of the most invisible professional institutions in our society, in that it has few nationally recognized leaders. . . . The demands and pressures on college presidents have become so great, and they must satisfy so many constituencies, that they have not been able to devote the time to developing that national visibility." "I believe I've been silent too long. . . . Presidents must take a leadership role in the public arena by expressing views on non-education issues." "[I feel] a yearning to have the courage to be as outspoken for social justice and social change as I was in the 60s and 70s. I feel badly that I have missed opportunities for civil leadership. I should write and speak more on issues important to a democratic society."

The giants for whom people express nostalgia were exceptional presidents whose voices were in the forefront of public discourse about education and public policy. Charles Eliot, Andrew White, Daniel Coit Gilman, James Angell, William Rainey Harper, David Starr Jordan, James Conant, and Robert Hutchins are most prominent. That these men were major public figures with national influence is irrefutable. However, the social, institutional, and personal circumstances that surrounded their presidencies were vastly different from the context of today's presidency.

Dramatic changes affecting the college presidency in what has been termed the "post-heroic age" have greatly circumscribed the president's public role.

Devaluation of leaders in society. A 1992 Louis Harris poll found that only 25 percent of the respondents said they had "a great deal of confidence" in people running universities, down from 61 percent in 1966. The decline of confidence in leaders is even greater in other areas: only 10 percent had a great deal of confidence in congressional leaders, 11 percent in law firms, 13 percent in the press, and 16 percent in the White House ("In-Box," 1992).

This devaluation of leaders has rendered college presidents more vulnerable to attacks from offended constituencies. College presidents of an earlier era commanded great respect, even awe, among the public and the media, and those who were outspoken felt independent enough to express bold ideas on complicated social, political, and economic issues. The lack of respect, trust, and confidence in leaders today vitiates a president's ability to make a difference.

Diminution of authority and autonomy in the college presidency. The respect, authority, independence, and longevity that earlier presidents enjoyed all were factors in freeing their public voice. Eliot served forty years at Harvard, as did Angell at Michigan. Presidential authority diminished in the early twentieth century as the American Association of University Professors (AAUP) organized, strengthening faculty prerogatives and assuring academic freedom for the professoriat. As faculty power increased, presidential power waned.

The average tenure of college and university presidents today is down to seven years (Ross, Green, and Henderson, 1993, p. ix). The lack of longevity and job security reduces the independence that frees a president to participate in public life. Many administrators today are concentrating on a low profile and personal survival; they have a sense of "being under constant observation—every speech, every letter, every policy decided" (Kerr and Gade, 1986, p. 28).

Increasing complexity of the presidency. Presidents today find themselves in thrall to multiple and unremitting internal and external demands and challenges. John Silber, one of the longest-serving presidents of the late twentieth century (twenty-five years at Boston University), compares the work of university presidents to that of big-city mayors, with the added complexities and constituencies of the academy (1989, pp. xii–xiii).

Faced with budget and enrollment problems, fundraising obligations, lobbying requirements, meetings, social events, campus crises, correspondence, phone calls, stacks of reading material, and faculty, staff, student, trustee, and community demands, presidents wearily contemplate the responsibilities and satisfactions of civic leadership.

Hutchins, who presided in a simpler era, forged a national reputation by accepting a hundred speaking engagements a year and publishing numerous articles in popular magazines and scholarly journals. However, he left his office at 5 P.M. every afternoon, never entertained or attended social functions in the evening, went to bed by 9 or 9:30 P.M., and thus was able to write every morning from 6 to 8 A.M. (Mayer, 1993, pp. 94, 178). Having freed himself from the relentless presidential schedule with weekend athletic events and countless social activities, Hutchins found ample time to read, write, and deliver speeches.

Another well-known president who made a similar choice is Father Theodore Hesburgh, who served thirty-five years at Notre Dame. When he accepted the presidency in 1952, Hesburgh decided never to attend parties or social events in South Bend. This is a virtually impossible choice for most college presidents, but one that enabled Hesburgh to devote time to public policy issues related to higher education, civil rights, international peace, immigration, and atomic energy. Hesburgh served on many committees and accepted numerous speaking engagements. His high visibility was good for Notre Dame's reputation, although he estimates it kept him away about one-third of the time (Hesburgh and Reedy, 1990, p. 73).

The challenge of administering today's higher education institutions is complicated by the varied groups and interests a president serves. Earlier presidents were likely to share a similar class, religion, gender, and world view with trustees, donors, and faculty. Being isomorphic with important constituencies gave those presidents the freedom to speak and act as they wished. In contrast, "presidents today find themselves at the fulcrum of conflicting constituencies, internal and external, and differing values, interests, priorities, and perspectives" (McLaughlin and Riesman, 1983, p. 183). Concern about alienating these diverse constituencies constrains the public voice and political action of today's college presidents.

Shift from entrepreneurial to administrative presidencies. The role of the college president has evolved from that of the colonial religious leader and moral arbiter to the entrepreneur of the post–Civil War research university and then to the institution builder of the post–World War II era. Today's administrative presidency is "that of a political leader . . . using persuasion in working with others to move in progressive ways and to keep conflict within reasonable bounds—working with media, with coalitions, and more publicly with bigger constituencies" (Kerr, 1991, p. 220). Inexorably, the presidency has changed as higher education and its social context have evolved, and the leaders of yore who are recalled with admiration would not do well at the helm of today's institutions. Trustees at the turn of the century sought leaders who were visionary, innovative, entrepreneurial, and authoritarian. These were the years of unprecedented growth and change in higher education as the private research and land-grant institutions emerged. We associate presidents from this era with major educational innovations. These presidents also served as public intellectuals, using the bully pulpit to engage a national audience with their ideas on education, social reform, and world affairs.

The context for leadership today is vastly different. This is the result of social and economic forces and also the maturing of higher education as a system. Higher education boards today do not seek innovators, entrepreneurs, or builders. Instead, they call on leaders with skill as consensus builders, administrators, fundraisers, and lobbyists to keep their institutions on course. In an era of fiscal constraints, changing demographics, public disaffection, and heated competition for resources and students, presidents are focused on maintaining the viability and quality of their institutions, which limits time for civic leadership.

Liberating the Public Voice of Presidents

Attacks on the failure of contemporary college presidents to act as public intellectuals reflect ignorance of both the changed circumstances surrounding the college presidency and the active public role taken by today's presidents in local civic affairs and national education policy. If the voice from the bully pulpit seems muted, my 1994 survey demonstrates that it is because presidents have little time to devote to reading, thinking, or writing, and because they are concerned about offending their constituencies and jeopardizing the neutrality of their institutions.

For college presidents, maintaining their institutions' reputation and neutrality must always be the litmus test by which public actions are measured. Derek Bok, former president of Harvard University, is a staunch advocate of institutional neutrality. He writes: "Presidents . . . must . . . refrain from using their authority to impose their private political views on the university. . . . Academic leaders are appointed to serve the interests of a wide variety of groups who support the university and benefit from its activities" (1982, p. 86).

Despite the constraints on today's presidents, there are those who do speak out on complex issues: Charles Young, University of California, Los Angeles, on affirmative action; Talbot D'Alemberte, Florida State University, on abortion rights; Claire Gaudiani, Connecticut College, on world poverty issues; and seventeen women college presidents in Massachusetts, on welfare reform. Other presidents who have been outspoken or active politically include Tom Kean at Drew University, John Silber at Boston University, Leon Botstein at Bard College, and Johnetta Cole at Spelman College.

The key to liberating a college president to serve society as a public intellectual is the explicit endorsement of that role by trustees and regents. Boards should recognize that, within limits, local and national leadership by college and university presidents enhances the reputation of an institution. In most president-board relationships, this aspect of the president's role is not discussed. More presidents could have a significant presence on the local, national, and world stages if their boards would sanction their public role, provide time for reading and writing, and stand behind them during public controversy.

In today's environment, a president's priorities must be enrollments, budgets, and endowments, for nothing so liberates a president as the confidence of a board satisfied that the institution is healthy and fiscally sound. Presidents owe their boards the assurance of good management; trustees owe their presidents the freedom and time to participate judiciously in public life without professional jeopardy. One of the presidential respondents to the survey believes that "a president and board should have a clear understanding on this, ideally before a president is hired." The public role of a president is an appropriate matter for discussion during the search and hiring process.

Once the college president secures the support of the board, a variety of public roles is possible. Presidents who enjoy special access to the media based on personal reputation or institutional prestige should use their favored position to command a national audience for their ideas. Other presidents should assert civic and intellectual leadership in their local communities. Presidents are best qualified to speak, write, and lobby on education-related issues. However, so much is at stake in the current debates about national policy on affirmative action, gun control, welfare, health care, the environment, the arts, and foreign policy that presidents are abdicating their responsibility as educated citizens if they fail to speak out.

Turning the corner of the new millennium, I believe that we should redefine and release the president as public intellectual. Presidents with expertise or strong, informed opinions on controversial national issues should be encouraged to speak out on them when a judicious voice might make a difference. The call to the presidency carries with it the responsibilities of civic leadership, and the bully pulpit provided by the position requires that presidents rise to those responsibilities.

References

Bender, T. *Intellect and Public Life: Essays on the Social History of Academic Intellectuals in the United States.* Baltimore: Johns Hopkins University Press, 1993.

Bok, D. *Beyond the Ivory Tower: Social Responsibilities of the Modern University.* Cambridge, Mass.: Harvard University Press, 1982.

Flawn, P. T. *A Primer for University Presidents: Managing the Modern University.* Austin: University of Texas Press, 1990.

Hesburgh, T. M., with Reedy, J. *God, Country, Notre Dame.* New York: Fawcett Columbine, 1990.

Honan, W. H. "At the Top of the Ivory Tower, the Watchword is Silence." *New York Times,* July 24, 1994, p. E5.

"In-Box." *Chronicle of Higher Education,* Apr. 15, 1992, p. A15.

Kerr, C. *The Great Transformation in Higher Education: 1960–1980.* Albany: State University of New York Press, 1991.

 C., and Gade, M. L. *The Many Lives of Academic Presidents: Time, Place and Character.* ington, D.C.: Association of Governing Boards of Universities and Colleges, 1986.

 , J. B., and Riesman, D. "The President: A Precarious Perch." In A. Levine (ed.), * ing in America, 1980–2000.* Baltimore: Johns Hopkins University Press, 1983.

Mayer, M. *Robert Maynard Hutchins: A Memoir.* Berkeley: University of California Press, 1993.
Ross, M., Green, M. F., and Henderson, C. *The American College President: A 1993 Edition.* Washington, D.C.: American Council on Education, 1993.
Silber, J. *Straight Shooting: What's Wrong with America and How to Fix It.* New York: Harper-Collins, 1989.

RITA BORNSTEIN is president of Rollins College in Winter Park, Florida.

New presidents are inundated with requests for their time, with the result that their private life is sacrificed for their job.

Finding a Balance

Milton A. Gordon, Margaret F. Gordon

The university presidency is like no other position in the academy. It has been my experience there is no accurate job description for the position and, as such, there is no true preparation. In fact, the expectations of the position vary greatly from campus to campus—and from time to time even on the same campus.

Although it is slowly changing, the average president comes to the position through the traditional route of professor and academic administrator—most frequently department chair, dean, or academic vice president. Having worked one's way up through the ranks, having spent the majority of one's professional career in academia, it would be logical to assume readiness. And to some extent that is true. There is familiarity with academic policies, theories, and the major issues in higher education, there is knowledge of university life, there is a vast library of literature to turn to for guidance—and there is certainly a plethora of consultants ready to provide advice on almost every conceivable issue. But what has been neglected for the most part is preparation for what, for want of a better term, may be called the personal side of being president. A sense of control over one's own time and the preservation of personal privacy, ironically two values that may have been deciding factors in becoming an academic in the first place, quickly take on the appearance of near-unattainable luxuries.

I am frequently asked about the differences in being a university president compared to other campus administrative positions. Several differences come readily to mind—the level of time commitment, the potentially all-consuming nature of the presidency, the conflicting views of the role of the president, and the involvement of the president's spouse and other family members.

From the first day on campus (indeed even before the first day on campus), the new president is inundated with invitations, meetings, and requests for speaking engagements. These requests come from every sector of the university and community—students, faculty, staff, alumni, politicians, business and corporate community members, and donors. Each sector has its own agenda and view of the role of the president. It quickly becomes apparent that it would be possible to be involved in activities literally seven days a week, twenty-four hours a day, and never meet all the expectations that have been placed upon the position of president. You soon come to the realization that wherever you are, you have said "no" to being somewhere else, at least once, and probably more than once. With every time commitment you make you have probably deviated from the view that one or more of your constituencies has of the proper role of a university president.

It becomes very important from the beginning to establish control over your schedule by setting some limits on the time you will be available. This is easier said than done. As a new president, there is a tendency to want to say yes. It is important to remember that to remain effective in the position, some personal time for you and your family must be maintained. In a recent article, the *Los Angeles Times* (Wallace, 1995) reported that when David Gardner was interviewed for the position of president for the University of California, he indicated that he would not work on Sundays and that he and his wife would not attend university functions more than two nights in a row. While these guidelines might not be appropriate for all presidents, some limits need to be established and this should be done at the outset of the presidency and made clear to all staff who control the schedule. This was something I learned the hard way. It is never too late to establish guidelines, but it is much more difficult once expectations have been established. It is important that some personal time be set aside for you and your family on a regular basis, and if it is not scheduled, it won't be available.

In addition to ensuring that the schedule allows for personal time, it is necessary to establish daily routines that take into account the varied aspects of the presidential role. This also is not always easy to achieve, particularly in light of the fact that the many constituencies of a university have widely differing views of the proper role of the president. Involvement in the daily operation of the university could easily consume the entire work day with the infinite number of phone calls, requests for meetings, and visitors who just stop in the office for a few seconds or minutes and stay until you indicate it is time to leave.

The daily routine should provide some time each day to keep abreast of larger educational issues. It is important that your schedule allow time to step back from the day-to-day operations of the university and to view higher education as a whole, to read and reflect upon state, regional, and national issues in higher education. This action is good for your own sanity and the sanity of those around you. Unfortunately, this time for reading and reflection is one of the easiest aspects to eliminate from a crowded schedule. There are many weeks when it is difficult not to be totally immersed in campus crises that seem to go on continuously. But by neglecting to include time for introspection and study, I feel that I'm not giving the campus and the higher education community what I really should—a balanced presidency.

Another important outcome from keeping current on issues in higher education is that it helps you realize that the campus issues with which you are confronted are not necessarily unique to your particular campus. There are issues that carry across to many, if not most of the other campuses similar to yours. This knowledge can be very helpful; it provides a potential resource for information and advice and also provides evidence that you are not the only person confronting a particular issue. Thus it tends to break down some of the isolation that presidents experience and to provide insight into your own daily operations and decisions.

I have found it helpful to schedule mornings working in my home office. This provides the quiet time for reading and reflection. The balance of the day is spent in the office or at meetings. I have also found it particularly helpful to establish a specific time each day to review the mail. One other caveat—on the rare occasions when a luncheon meeting has not been scheduled, get out of the office.

Each president must decide what is the appropriate balance among the various aspects of the position for his or her university. To be successful, a president must base this decision not only on his or her individual interests but also on the culture and custom of the university. There are university presidents who take an outside view of their presidencies, they are totally involved with national, regional, and state issues, and spend very little time on campus with the day-to-day operations of the university; there are also university presidents who take the opposite approach and view their presidencies as an inside position and are totally involved and immersed in the day-to-day operations of the campus. Both extremes can be successful if the approach matches the expectations of the majority of the constituencies. Most presidents probably fall somewhere between the two extremes and attempt to balance the various aspects of the position. Every president, however, must make his or her own decision in terms of the schedule and which aspects of the presidency are going to get the major time, energy, and emphasis.

It is important to physically get away from the position on a regular basis. With the advent of mobile phones, pagers, and portable computers, the campus and the community have access to you twenty-four hours a day, seven days a week. This actually has advantages and disadvantages. If you control technology rather than letting technology control you, it provides a way for you to be in communication with the campus when necessary without always being physically present in the office. If you don't have a way to get away, it can cause harm to you as a person and to your family. In my case, my wife and I have a cabin in the mountains about two hours' drive from where we live. We go there as frequently as we can because as we go up the mountain, the responsibilities and obligations of the presidency seem to slip away. We recognized a need for some retreat within the first year and our cabin has worked well for us.

It is recommended that long weekends occasionally be scheduled for mini vacations, which provide a break in the routine. The average time in office for a university president continues to become shorter and is now about five years. There is a high burnout rate among university presidents. Several recent events during the past few years have brought national attention to this. As a result, a few universities have begun to allow (or even insist) that presidents periodically go on paid leaves to study, travel, and catch up on the latest developments in their disciplines. This action is similar to a faculty sabbatical. In my opinion this will prove to benefit everyone. The profession benefits because it will keep the best and the brightest from burning out and leaving. The university benefits because it will be able to keep a president for a longer time, which may result in stability and also means the university will not have to conduct a costly and time-consuming search every few years and go through the learning period with a new president. Students and faculty benefit because they will be working with a president who knows the culture and the history of the university.

Once you become president, since everyone on campus, in essence, reports to you, you no longer have the luxury of close confidantes at the campus because you have the final evaluation, that is, the final decision in terms of their own position and well-being. This is one of the reasons, in spite of the busy schedule, for a sense of isolation about the presidency. I've come to recognize and respect and realize the need for national associations for presidents because of this isolation. This sense of isolation applies also to the family of the president, which may be in a somewhat ambivalent position. The spouse and children may be viewed as representatives of or conduits to the president and thus feel they are under some constraints in establishing personal relationships.

Privacy is at a premium—and even more so if there is a presidential home. There are many advantages to a presidential home—entertaining is more convenient, the campus feels more involved, and I believe it is easier to develop closer relationships between the president and the various on- and off-campus constituencies. These advantages have corresponding disadvantages: loss of privacy, a campus sense of ownership, and the expectation of a greater level of entertaining and use of the home for campus functions. Again, it is important to set limits at the outset. Expectations differ from campus to campus but the family will be more involved if you have a presidential home.

If you have the opportunity to provide input into the design of the presidential home, make sure the architect pays attention to establishing separate public and private quarters. We learned of the importance of maintaining separate private quarters the hard way. When we moved into the El Dorado Ranch, the university home, in August 1990, we unpacked our personal belongings and placed them throughout the home. That was a mistake. Over the course of five years, as caterers have come in and out of the kitchen facilities, as large numbers of guests have gone through the home, many of these personal belongings have been broken or have disappeared. I strongly recommend that any president moving into a university home be cautious about commingling personal items with those for public or state use in the home. If it is at all possible, I recommend that the state or university purchase items for use in the public areas of the home to avoid the loss of personal belongings.

I believe I am fortunate that our university home is not on the grounds of the university. Even though we are very close, we are several miles from the campus, and it is easier to maintain a sense of privacy; there are those moments when you can have some personal time. But even though we are somewhat distant from the campus, it is difficult to truly be away because campuses tend to feel that the university home belongs to them and that just as the university library, office, and classroom buildings, the university home should be readily accessible to the campus. Frequently there is not the realization that people actually live there and have lives apart from the roles they perform for the campus. This is one of the reasons we have our mountain cabin. Not only does it provide a retreat and a sense of privacy, it also provides a home that is truly ours to do with as we please.

The upkeep of a presidential home may pose difficulties. I recommend any president, prior to accepting a position that includes a university home, ensure there is an endowment to maintain the home. A major part of the average president's time is now taken up with fundraising. However, it is very difficult to raise funds for a home in which you are going to reside. An endowment should contain sufficient funds to provide the home with all necessary furnishings, including kitchen utensils and glassware and their replacement on an ongoing basis; and funds for the physical upkeep and maintenance of the home. Many of the homes given to universities are old and are in need of frequent maintenance and repair. Even when the building is in good shape, funds are necessary for help to maintain the house and grounds on a daily basis and when events are scheduled.

I began my comments by suggesting there is no clear job description, no common set of expectations for a university president. This is even more true for the spouse of the president. The spouse is frequently interviewed along with the president. But the spouse is not the person hired, and the role of the spouse is ambiguous. The responsibilities that he or she is expected to fulfill as presidential spouse are unclear, varying from campus to campus, and also among the various constituencies on the same campus. In addition, there is less support for the presidential spouse in assuming his or her new role. There are a number of seminars established to assist presidents when they begin a new presidency. I would suggest that the potential impact of the presidency on the spouse and other family members be a standard topic in such seminars and that the spouse be included as a seminar participant if he or she wishes.

One of the major social changes in recent years has been the increase in the percentage of working spouses. This is also true for the families of university presidents and is a potential source of difficulty. Many spouses have established professional careers and attempt to juggle the commitments to their own professions with the commitments and expectations placed upon them as presidential spouses. Other spouses have found it necessary to give up their own careers to accompany the president. In both instances, the presidency places an additional strain on the family and this needs to be recognized and accommodated. For example, close friends of ours have established the first hour of every morning as inviolable time together. Others have established "date" nights. Whatever routine or method of accommodation is established, it is necessary that the importance of the family and its relationships be maintained.

Both my wife and I have professional positions in higher education; however, my wife also has a role as the spouse of the president. She enjoys the activities and the events with which she is involved on the campus and in the community and I believe the campus appreciates the fact that we view the presidency as a couple and work as a couple in the presidency. However, it has been necessary to establish clear limits to enable her to balance the commitments of her dual roles.

Although the spouse of the university president may have a number of obligations, he or she does not necessarily receive the acknowledgment or the support provided to the president and frequently receives little appreciation or recognition for his or her efforts. If not careful, the spouse may become someone that people enjoy having present—a benefit to any function—but also take for granted. The importance of the spouse's contribution may easily go unrecognized. The university should have established procedures that routinely acknowledge the contributions of the spouse and that enable the spouse to be involved to the degree to which he or she chooses. I have heard of instances at universities where if there is not a spouse, or even if there is a spouse but he or she is professionally occupied, the university actually hires someone to fill in to support the president because it is a much-needed position for a successful campus and presidency.

There is a tendency to ignore the personal aspects of being a president. But they can not be ignored for too long if we are to be successful in our professional lives. As my friend and colleague Bill Stacy, CSU San Marco, said, we need to remind ourselves to take care of ourselves and our families—something we are not known to be any good at.

A few simple rules can go a long way in ensuring a balance between your personal and professional lives: make time for yourself, your spouse, your family and friends; establish control over your schedule; establish a daily routine that includes time for all aspects of the presidency; establish, in conjunction with the culture of the university and your personal interests, where you will place your emphasis in the presidency; establish procedures that recognize the contributions of your spouse and family; if a presidential home is included, keep the business and personal aspects of living in the home separate as much as possible; and remember above all to enjoy yourself and have fun.

Reference

Wallace, A., "UC President Will Inherit System's Woes." *Los Angeles Times,* June 15, 1995, p. A3.

MILTON A. GORDON *is president of California State University, Fullerton.*

MARGARET F. GORDON *is dean of extended education at California State University, Dominguez Hills.*

A framework is given for setting the vision of new leadership during the first two years of the presidency, with time frames and tasks to engage the community in its future.

Developing a Vision

Claire Gaudiani

New presidents. They fill campuses with hope but also dread. They arrive flush with new ideas, great expectations, and their own night terrors. The new president's vision conveys to widely diverse constituencies a spirit of confidence about the future and enthusiasm for the new leadership. The "vision thing" becomes a key to success. What does the president see? Can others see it too? Can they move to make the vision a reality?

In sixth grade we all read that Constantine saw a vision for his army—a sign in the sky whose letters said, "In hoc signum, vinces." And in that sign, they did conquer. His soldiers were convinced of their leader's vision and fought effectively, knowing the outcome in advance. Oh for the days when the leader's view of the future was so powerful! Constantine did not have diverse constituencies or polls to contend with.

Today, most leaders really have to engage their constituencies, to evoke, as well as announce, a vision of the future. Stone Soup is now a better model for vision setting. In this Russian folktale, three hungry, tired soldiers arrive in a village as they make their way home after an unnamed war. They go from house to house seeking some bread, but each villager claims that the postwar cupboards are bare, that even the townspeople are starving, so there is nothing extra for strangers.

In despair, the soldiers go to the town square. One of them suddenly announces that he will have to make Stone Soup, and he asks to borrow a cauldron and water. Curious onlookers bring these items, and watch while the soldiers locate one fine large round stone—a zesty soup stone. Others gather wood quickly and bring embers to light the fire. As the water comes to a boil, a ladle is offered for the first tasting. The lead soldier congratulates the growing crowd on the excellent soup stones they have in their town. Pleased and proud, townspeople draw closer to the strangers and respond quickly when the soldiers suggest that a carrot and a potato would bring out the rich stone flavor. More vegetables, and then soup bones and a joint or two, arrive, and then other villagers bring contributions, as well. By nightfall, the hearty soup is ready, and it feeds the whole village their richest and happiest meal since long before the war.

In this story, soldiers had a vision—a good, hearty, peaceful dinner for themselves. They made their vision a reality, but also achieved much more—a fine dinner for the entire village, a strong and positive community experience, and a lesson for the villagers in how generosity and cooperation can improve life for everyone. They succeeded in making their vision a reality, not by announcing their vision, but by capturing the imagination of the villagers with an intriguing idea—Stone Soup. Moreover, their efforts began by locating the most important ingredient right there in the village—the large fine round soup stone. The process that followed was really a seduction—the villagers gradually falling for the idea of stone soup and deciding to participate in making it by giving something of their very own; something they had previously resisted sharing. The soldiers' vision and the experience they organized enabled the villagers to see and value their village assets quite differently. In fact, they became motivated to risk bringing some of those items out of the recesses of their cupboards, because they began to see how they could become more important in the cauldron than they were in the cupboard. The new president's vision should likewise entice the community to engage and give individual gifts to the common good.

A close reader of this story might object to its relevance to the experience of the new college president in at least four important ways. The soldiers did not come through a search process, were not selected to lead the village, and had no mandate and no power of an office to make things happen. However, while the soldiers did just arrive in town, for most people, so does the new president. In fact, in most cases this is exactly how campus villagers perceive the new president, although the president may not understand this for years. She and her vision have not been searched for or eagerly awaited by the community—only by the search committee and a few dozen others. The search itself has meant little to the majority of the community, except as passing curiosity. Of course, the trustees may have a mandate in mind but they are not on campus daily. The real villagers rarely have a compelling mandate they hope the new president will pursue. Some, perhaps most, just hope that, in their area, things do not change too much.

Finally—though it may not seem so—the president, like the soldiers, cannot really force change in attitude. In fact, it is no understatement to say that presidents of academic institutions have no more real power to exert over the faculty, staff, students, and alumni than the soldiers had over the villagers. Power is like fuel, anyway; if you use it, you lose it, and you may lose other things, as well. Imagine if the soldiers had decided to use their power to break into homes and take the food they wanted, or take hostages and force the villagers to give up their food in order to get the hostages back. Those soldiers would not have had a good day, a good dinner, or a safe continuation of their journey. Most presidents know not to break and enter their new institution, but many make their first round of visits on campus and find the villagers polite but the cupboards bare. They hear good explanations outlining why things are the way they are. It may occur to the new president that realization of the vision will have to involve force. How about some powerful statements about cost-containment and accountability? Maybe the president should appoint a team to replan the university? Maybe hire a consultant for advice.... But if the new president is wise like the soldiers, she will see that what she really needs is a way to capture the imagination of the community.

The imaginative, even seductive, engagement of people in a fresh way of seeing the world is the first step of vision setting. The announcement of "Stone Soup" contains the president's vision and the power to make it a reality because the concept is open and engaging. It recognizes that power and resources are in the community itself—not in the president. The new vision is not a list of three, five, or fifteen presidential initiatives. Those will look like complicated add-on jobs for a lot of already busy people and they will make the president look like everybody's problem and nobody's solution, like the source of new burdens. The new vision should free people to see their own opportunity to contribute to an appealing project. One of the keys to a successful presidency is understanding how little power you have over people, yet what enormous power you have over their imagination. The role of the vision is to connect the knowledge and skills of the president and the community so powerfully that an outcome well beyond what anyone could have imagined actually results.

Like the soldiers, the new president has three distinct time frames in which to build a powerful vision to motivate the institution's community. The arrival in town or naming of the new president; the inauguration, when the vision is announced and first tastings occur; and the first two years where the soup is made and dinner is served.

Vision Setting: From Appointment to First Day on the Job

A magical and commonly underutilized period occurs between the announcement of the new president's name and the moment the new leader arrives on campus to take the helm. The trajectory toward success or failure is often set during these months. The announcement itself focuses everyone's attention on every word, smile, raised eyebrow, and head toss of the new president. Each is read for hidden meaning. This is the time for the president to capture the imagination of the community and to begin to set the vision and the style of the new era.

Mutterings . . .

"Will things get better for the faculty at last . . . or get worse?" "Are we finally going to have someone who can control costs . . . or get the faculty in line, or not?" "Is our college's reputation finally going to return to the high level we alums remember . . . or not?"

The new president's first informal remarks to the community and the press initiate a critical process of sizing up the leader and hopes for the future. These remarks and subsequent presentations on and off campus should show a true grasp of the institution's history. Good research and preparation for candidate interviews will have indicated some of the nuggets, but it is even worth delaying the announcement for a few days if the president can have the archivist, the secretary to the board of trustees, or other trusted insiders to the search process collect some stories about the institution's past, its heroes and heroines, historic moments, and decisions in which the community takes pride. People will move forward with greater energy and confidence with a leader who knows and values their shared past. Telling the institution's best stories reduces the profile of the new president as an outsider. Knowledge of the history shows respect for the institution, humility, thoughtfulness, and a willingness to do more work than is necessary. These are some of the virtues a leader needs in order to lead well, and ones most presidents probably have; if the community can discover them firsthand, some fears will be allayed.

Overheard . . .

"Is he arrogant?" "Does she care about this place or is she using us as a career stepping stone?" "Am I going to like this president?" "Why did they choose him?" "Why did she decide to accept this position?"

The prehoneymoon, preinaugural period is also a time to listen and establish the style of a listening leader. My dear great aunt who taught nursing in the 1920s once told me that people know what is right and what is wrong with them. They even know something about how to get better. Most doctors do not listen, do not ask, and do not watch carefully enough to learn. My aunt's wisdom applies to institutions, both big and small. The new president can only benefit from listening to the people. She will, after all, be setting the new vision, new directions, and new expectations, and certainly knows the external conditions impinging on the institution better than most community members. For the new vision to be seen quickly in the community and at many different levels, the people need to believe they have helped to shape it. In fact, the president's vision will be powerfully enriched by its contact with the wisdom of the community.

Listening can also demonstrate the president's values and style. After my appointment, in the five months before I assumed the presidency of Connecticut College, I announced in the campus newspaper that, every ten days, I would be on campus for a full day of community consultations. I asked all members of the community to come talk with me, to let me know what I needed to know to lead the college well. I asked people to bring any papers or reports they thought would help me understand our past and plan for our future. Because I believe that valuable insights come from people at all levels of the college community, and that encouraging creativity and responsibility for the common good among all community members multiplies institutional assets, I made certain that custodians and secretaries, faculty and students, directors and deans all felt welcome to sign up for a half hour with me.

This was some of the most valuable time of my early years as president. I had a chance to get to know so many different people, to hear their stories, hopes, and disappointments, and to receive their warnings and suggestions. I prefaced each meeting by stressing that these meetings were not for me to talk or to make promises or commitments, but to listen and learn. I assured each person confidentiality and took notes after asking if the visitor was comfortable with my note taking. I read notes back to assure both of us that I had really heard the messages. I asked questions, many questions that helped me to test new ideas, to gauge reactions to current conditions, to connect what I had read in the catalogues, handbooks, and histories to the human dimension at the college. My closing questions to each person were: "What values do you think most people share on this campus?" "What one change would be most powerful for you, your colleagues, and the school?" (Even now, seven years later, I continue to use this style of consultation from time to time as I face important decisions.)

The president's willingness to listen not only brings in a lot of information and wisdom, but also demonstrates her values and style and buys goodwill. Many people see themselves as leaders in an academic setting. Consulting with the new president gives these people a chance to shape her thinking and to feel their own leadership. In addition, frequently repeated ideas begin to have deeper meaning for the president and she can acknowledge these ideas, making people feel good about their meetings with her.

Reflections . . .

"We used to always . . . but now we. . . ." "In this campus with all the people who . . . we ought to be able to. . . ." "When . . . was here, a lot of us were excited that the college was going to . . . but then. . . ." "A lot of us would be willing to work pretty hard to . . . but we would need. . . ."

Finally, listening familiarizes the campus with the new president. It gives many different people personal time with her. They recount their experiences to others. As members of all constituent groups start to evolve a clearer sense of who this new president really is, she becomes less of a stranger. This process diminishes the chance that any one incident or the opinion of any one person can be determinative, particularly negatively determinative.

Meetings like these should continue as open office hours for faculty, staff, and students every few weeks through the president's first year and subsequently, if possible. The president's personal engagement with people sets an important example for everyone who supervises others about how to listen, how to care, how to evolve vision, eventually set goals, evaluate achievements and value people.

Vision Setting: Between First Day and Inauguration

From the first full day of official responsibility to the day of the inaugural, the president has a chance to connect what she learned in the community consultations with her own insights about higher education, change, and the role of the institution under new leadership.

The president's ideas are, of course, vital to vision setting. She was, after all, chosen from a competitive group because of strengths that a cross-section of people on the search committee thought were just what the institution needed. A collective wisdom was already applied to address the question of what the new vision should be and the answer is the new leader.

The months between arrival on campus and inauguration are a powerful time to engage the official governance structures in thinking about the future. The president's question at this point is: "What do you think we need to do to dramatically strengthen our institution?" The president should begin to engage the formal governance structure, much as she had engaged informally with individuals earlier. Convening trustees, faculty, staff, and student and alumni leaders in separate groups, the president should address this question with people in half-day and even daylong retreats. Rather than trying to solve any problems, these meetings should aim to get ideas out on the table. With the president asking the questions, and a scribe recording ideas on flip charts, these brainstorming sessions can release new energies and freshen perspectives. With minimum guidance from the president, each constituency engaging the question will identify institutional strengths and weaknesses and identify information needed to assess these more fully and to forecast the risks and opportunities which lie ahead. The president's role is to liberate fresh thinking and to encourage blue-sky speculation. After six or seven of these constituent-based meetings, the president can ask two people from each group to go through all the notes and papers from the individual meetings and collect the ideas that recurred in two or more meetings.

Cross-sectional leadership meetings should follow the constituent group meetings to share outcomes developed. At these meetings with leadership collected from a cross-section of faculty, staff, students, and, if possible, alumni, the president can read back to the assembled group what the institutional leadership has said it believes, fears, and aspires to become. In all of these meetings, the president can keep testing parts of her own vision and verifying the wisdom gleaned in the earlier informal community consultations. The mix of the president's initial vision, the informal consultations, and the formal brainstorming are critical to the rich soup the president is simmering. The new president can ask more questions, and suggest some areas for further research but not really unveil the vision—that is for the inauguration. It is widely reassuring for everyone to discover the rich overlap in understanding shared by members of different constituencies. It is also good to unearth widely held notions that may in fact, be mistaken. At one college, the president heard, "To make this a stronger college, we would have to pay women faculty better. Everyone knows women faculty are paid less here for the same rank and number of years of service than men." The president's question was, "Have we done a study to prove this? No? We need to do the study, then." When a study was done, this assertion proved false and correct information could be shared.

These meetings are powerful signs that the president will lead *with* the community, that the community has had informal and formal shaping effect on the new president, and that fundamentally they will be able to trust the new vision because it is already "ours," not an isolated "hers." The community has watched the vision being made. Finally, the vision, inclusive and responsive as it is likely to be, can be announced at the inauguration.

I always worry when new presidents say they will take the first year or so to really learn about the institution before making any big pronouncements. The president loses valuable honeymoon time that can never be recaptured. The college loses the momentum that a change in leadership releases. And chances are that the president will have to make a difficult and potentially divisive decision before having captured the institution's imagination, engaged its best resources on its own behalf, or increased the community's confidence in their new leader or increased their collective sense of well-being. Energetic use of the two early time periods enables a decisive vision to emerge early in the president's tenure, take hold strongly, and stand as a protective shield between the president and the first dangerous moment.

Inauguration: Laying Out the Vision

The inauguration itself should capture the future of the institution in courageous ways. The community anticipates a fresh perspective from the new president's inaugural. The address should recognize external conditions, build on the strengths of the institution, and strike in new directions that have been shaped by the president's vision and the consultations with various constituencies. People should hear clearly what the president values and what the institution will be striving for, but they will treasure hearing, as well, the value the president places on the institution's own history and internal wisdom. The president's vision should be shaped and worded in ways that the various constituencies can understand and own. Citing the wise words of an emeritus professor or kitchen staffer to illustrate a point, referencing a moment of institutional history, the president confirms that careful homework and listening has followed the announcement of the new leader. The vision expressed in the inauguration should become a point of reference for the president's tenure. As years pass, people should be able to go back to that speech and recognize it as the map for the journey the president has led.

The address itself connects past with future, insiders and old-timers with newcomers and new-thinkers. Respecting the past gives the new president extra leeway to focus on his or her new vision, personal style and stamp, favorite references, unique moral commitments. People will be more willing to accept the new president's vision if its first public presentation marks it as organically connected to the best of the past and striving ambitiously to create the best future for the institution. To keep the vision clear:

Don'ts
Don't begin sentences with "When I was at . . . "
Don't point out weaknesses of the institution or its past leaders—no matter what.
Don't forget that you symbolize the college and its values and commitments, and that you represent authority—but must tread softly to move effectively.
Don't be small-minded, easily hurt, or vengeful.

Do's
Do take in what new colleagues tell you, and work from the college's strengths with discretion.
Do have open office hours for *all* staff, students, faculty, and so on—and have lunch in garage with physical plant personnel.
Do thank widely: not just trustees and major donors, but faculty, students, and staff in the kitchen and physical plant as well as directors and vice presidents. After graduation or reunion, for instance, write notes. Ask faculty and supervisors to let you know when someone they work with deserves special thanks.
Do take time to repair your spirit and keep checking on the vision.

After Inauguration: Confirming and Achieving the Vision

Most communities divide into three groups after the inaugural: believers, skeptics, and same-old-same-olds or wait-and-seers. The believers are those whose imagination the president has captured early or perhaps those whose jobs depend most closely on the president's approval. They may be the naturally optimistic or enthusiastic people who must almost be actively dissuaded from a positive view of the future. The skeptics are those who have decided that this leader cannot or probably will not succeed, or that no leadership ever really succeeds, or that fundamentally all authority is corrupt. The rest are the people who have seen presidents come and go and know that life will go on as usual regardless; that no one, certainly not they, need change or engage . . . probably.

The president's postinaugural task is to engage the believers deeply in the vision, make the same-olds into believers and move the skeptics into the wait-and-see category. To work this magic, the president can proceed with three or more of the following steps:

Address a long-standing need decisively. In one university, the informal and formal early consultative processes indicated that benefits had become a sore point for faculty and staff. Two days after the inauguration, the new president assembled a cross-departmental team including faculty and staff to explore and address employee benefits issues. The charge to the task force was constructed using the president's notes from preinauguration individual and group meetings. The task force was given a ten-week period to complete the work, and the human resources head and institutional research director were both on the team, along with two hourly employees, two salaried staff, and four faculty, one of whom chaired the task force. They gathered annual comparative data from the institution's past and from a set of peer institutions, made cost and revenue projections, and established a deeper understanding of a broad range of issues related to benefits. While comprehensive participatory strategic planning was proceeding on schedule, this widely perceived problem that the community had shared with the new president was moving ahead on a faster track, thus satisfying people that straightforward progress could be made on previously identified issues.

In addition, the president used this issue to model how to make change. The president had assembled a widely representative community-based team, given it a clear charge and time frame, and provided access to all relevant data. The president met with the team every three weeks to hear progress and advice. He offered additional sources of information, suggested ways to phase in changes, and encouraged people to use benefits more wisely and reduce costs. The way this work proceeded briskly, addressed a major issue for all employees, and merited the president's personal attention, gave clear signals that the new president not only listened well (consultative period) and spoke well (the inauguration) but could act decisively and not just on issues he cared about. He showed that he could commit resources, including his own time, to issues the community brought forward. Thus, he also modeled how others could step forward and commit to work on issues he considered of strategic importance.

Identify and achieve one success in the new vision. Early successes capture people's imagination and release energies for the new efforts ahead. At one college, the new president's vision proposed that the institution define itself more clearly by a Center for Leadership Studies. Within her first year as president, she was able to induce a donor to endow a chair for this center. After that, the rest of her vision seemed achievable. "She had, after all, brought in the chair for . . . " In another case, the president wanted to initiate a new international initiative that required two faculty votes. Getting legislation composed and passed within the first six months of the president's first year was seen as a first-order triumph and suggested that other curricular changes might be possible as well—in a setting that had experienced prolonged stalemate on academic change. The extra time and effort that these new presidents expended on their early successes paid substantial dividends for years.

Develop a broadly participatory and comprehensive planning process. The president's vision for distinctive institutional strength should be presented in crisp, courageous, and memorable form in the inaugural, but when participatory, comprehensive planning is a part of the vision, the institution's doors and windows remain open to more possibilities. People feel that their advising and the president's listening have connected to create hopes and dreams beyond those the search committee saw. The wait-and-seers and same-olds will be likely to pay attention. Even skeptics might take note. The inaugural can make it clear that a full planning process will be necessary to build the institution to new strengths.

Often, new presidents approach planning by appointing a committee to write an institutional plan focusing on the central ideas of the president's vision as they have been agreed upon loosely by trustees or articulated in a more isolated vision statement at the inauguration. "Our university will take a national leadership role in advancing research while improving undergraduate education, utilize new technologies throughout the curriculum, and strengthen our ties to the local community as one of our great assets." The team now has its mandate—how best can we progress on making this vision real?

This kind of planning can be a major stumbling block. The problem with this approach is how many people are left off center stage without a role to play, before they even know how they feel about the new director. Options begin to close down for many faculty, students, and staff. "Well, I guess the arts are not part of the president's vision. . . ." "The president is not concerned about scholarships, diversity, or the quality of student life or. . . ." How much better it is to announce three broad areas that are the core of the vision of a stronger and striving institution and announce *as part of the vision* that a powerful participatory planning effort will engage hundreds of community members.

A comprehensive planning process will lay open the whole institution to change, not just the three or four pet areas of concern to the new president. "From this comprehensive effort at reenvisioning the future together, we will discover and invent new strengths and remember old ones!" The president can follow words like these by referring to two or more most often repeated ideas from the earlier consultations as areas for consideration by the planning process.

Establish systematic management systems. Vision without a plan is pie in the sky, not nourishing soup. The systematic management of tasks and teams within crisp time frames is critical to achieving the vision. New presidents quickly reveal their management styles and these influence the way their vision is perceived by others.

Continued Muttering . . .

"He is great on details, loses the forest for the trees." "Great conceptualizer and visionary but forget trying to get an answer to a question in finite time, never mind by a deadline." "Likes to give assignments . . . can't be counted on to complete any."

Hardworking staff, especially those closest to the president, are the canaries in the mine where the president's vision is hidden. People will look to them to see how well they look as they work hard closest to the new vision. Systematic dependable management of tasks assures their health, productivity, and good feelings about their work. It also bolsters the confidence of those who watch them. Constant frustration with confusing and unclear signals, missed deadlines, scrambled prioritizations or volatile reprioritizations show in the eyes and sighs of the president's staff. The unmistakable danger signs are clear to others.

Solutions are available. Management software packages can enable the president and senior administrators to track projects efficiently. They are well worth the investment. The software helps assure that routine updates on projects or problems can be exchanged by computer and only take up meeting time if special circumstances suggest it. To manage the paper flow among and between senior staff and the president, I mark documents with initials of staff who should get copies and add R.D. to indicate that a response is due. At our regularly scheduled meetings, the senior administrators and I go through their sets of papers. Both of us are already well prepared to discuss them. I also periodically review the senior administrators' operational and strategic objectives to be sure that they and we are staying the course. These periodic reviews of the major goals occur while the R.D. files and software printouts assure that the rest of the range of responsibility is covered in appropriate detail and in predictable time frames.

Systematic management means thinking ahead of the schedule of activities so that deadlines are met without pressuring colleagues unnecessarily. The president's management style should include enabling senior administrators to forecast their work clearly, paving the steps from the event or the goal backward to "the work we need to do today." Reviewing schedules systematically with senior administrators will enable the president to connect elements of his or her vision to the daily unfolding of the first year. A new president will need last year's calendar of events for each constituency (students, faculty, trustees), curricular change schedules, and information and dates for each important college process (for example, the tenure process). Systematic management of tasks and time makes for easier leadership of people, and assures that the president's vision is not pie in the sky, but a real treasure that all will benefit from.

Learn names, learn names, learn names—everyone's. Finally, through the first year, the vision will be as real to people as they believe they are to the new president. The president needs to learn names. People know the president and his or her ideas belong to the institution and belong in the institution when the president makes people belong in his or her mind. To make the vision accepted by people, accept them as distinct individuals—learn their names. The new president will be expecting a lot of individuals to invest time and energy beyond the call of duty. The personal touch of knowing names early is deeply appreciated and admired because it is so hard. The president needs to show the self-discipline of doing something hard that is a gesture of consideration for others if she wants the same energy back in the offices, classrooms, labs, libraries, and on the fields and grounds of the campus.

Conclusion

Setting the vision is the president's most dramatic, difficult, and interesting work in the first year or two in office. The success of this task often determines the length and strength of the president's tenure and the contribution that tenure makes, not only to the institution as a whole, but just as importantly to the professional growth and personal well-being of the individuals who comprise the institution, including the president herself.

Each time the president models open, dynamic, courageous, disciplined, and inclusive thinking, people learn how to create similar environments in their own offices, departments, and workplaces. Over time, the spirit of the institution may come to reflect the style and spirit of the president. It can also reflect the institution's reaction against that style and spirit. The process of vision setting takes time and is very similar, even in diverse institutional educational settings. Ultimately, the vision is about the institution imagining itself, and it is about the president teaching the community to make and share its future, well-being, and success.

CLAIRE GAUDIANI is president and professor of French literature at Connecticut College in New London, Connecticut.

Instead of searching for some mythic Ideal President, we need to reclaim reality and think seriously about the core tasks of leadership.

Demystifying the Presidency

Robert Hahn

This chapter casts a net broadly, posing questions and suggesting some answers about presidential leadership. The general approach is in keeping with my theme of collective responsibility and is also in line with my career-long interest in the topic of leadership. I can trace this interest back to my earliest days as a classroom teacher, when my texts were the leadership sagas of Oedipus Rex and King Lear, through a stint as an author of case studies, to my work as director of a management institute. Now the edge of that interest is sharper still, because I have become case-study fodder myself.

After years as faculty member, department chair, and chief academic officer, I joined the ranks of college presidents, and at this writing, I am in my fifth year as president of a state college. I have found the experience of the presidency to be one whose challenges, burdens, and rewards are unique.

I remember serving on an accreditation team, when I was an academic dean, and hearing one of my fellow team members, a financial officer, observe, "I can't imagine why so many people get bitten by the presidential bug, when the job is a year of exhilaration followed by a lifetime of heartbreak." But this financial officer has since become a president himself, testifying that if his hyperbole has a grain of verity, as it does, the whole truth is different. The whole truth is . . . well, put it this way. If a new president were asking me for advice today, I would say, above all, take pleasure in the fact that you now have one of the most fascinating, endlessly stimulating jobs in the world. Every day that you live as a president will be a day lived in interesting times. (In addition,

---

A version of this chapter called "Getting Serious About Presidential Leadership: Our Collective Responsibility" was published in *Change*, September/October 1995, volume 27, number 5, pp. 12–20.

I do have some more specific advice to offer a new president, which I will hold for my conclusion.)

Does the Ideal President Exist?

In issue after issue of the *Chronicle of Higher Education,* we read of another troubled presidency, another leader worn down or driven out, in distress or under fire. The stories are complemented by ads for presidential searches, seeking candidates with demonstrated success as leaders, including strength in administration, scholarship, and curriculum; a track record in fiscal management and fundraising; prowess in recruitment, motivation, and supervision; knowledge of technology and collective bargaining; mastery of communications and public relations (with communities, businesses, legislatures); sensitivity and commitment (to a swelling list of ideals, issues, and special interests); skill in consensus building and strategic planning . . . not to mention creativity, imagination, and, yes, vision.

Question: Although we seek leaders who have demonstrated success in these areas and more, the tales of imploding presidencies suggest that many have failed to demonstrate any success at all, let alone success gauged by godlike criteria. If this is so, if failure is endemic in the ranks of presidents, then where are the leaders who can measure up to our standards of success?

The answer is that they don't exist. They are like Shakespeare's Antony in Cleopatra's vision of him:

CLEOPATRA: His legs bestrid the ocean, his reared arm
 Crested the world. His voice was propertied
 As all the tuned spheres. . . .
 Think you there was, or might be, such a man
 As this I dreamt of?
DOLABELLA: Gentle madam, no.

Adjusted for gender, the statement about Antony applies to our collective longing for the Ideal President. The problem is not that the Antony of Cleopatra's imagination doesn't exist. The problem is that *we believe* such a person could exist. As long as we believe this—that heroes on chargers can sweep down from the west and solve intractable problems with dazzling strokes of invention—we participate in myth making, and we fail to confront the problem: why we find it difficult to identify, develop, and sustain successful presidential leaders. Our mythic thinking, wistful and evasive at best, sloppy and myopic at worst, makes us culpable. If presidential leadership is a problem, we are a major part of that problem.

There will be more successful presidents when we are able to think more seriously about what we need from them, and about the conditions that enable their success. We need to be less superficial in our thinking about leadership. We need to consider our own collective role, as citizens, in the successful governance of our institutions. This means giving up some of our more simplistic notions of success. It means looking beneath the surfaces and behind the images.

Although this sounds straightforward, it is a challenge, because we dote on surfaces and oversimplifications; we delight in images and sound bites; and we are, it seems, critics by nature—we love to weigh our leaders in the balance and find them wanting. What we should be is an engaged community of thoughtful citizens. What we have become is an audience, bedazzled or dismissive by turns—too easily beguiled or too quick to boo the performer off the stage.

Granted, it isn't only us—our presidents also contribute to image mongering and superficial thinking. As an illustration, consider that phenomenon known as "The New President's Workshop." There are dozens of these, short and long, free and expensive, ranging from the anecdotal to the theoretical. Some, like Harvard's summer workshop, have real depth, while others are like sessions on improving your golf swing.

These offer tips from the pros and insider advice ranging from the ominous ("Don't trust the first people who approach you!") to the comic ("Don't let the food service use those ugly yellow glasses in your house!"), and include such advice as "Seem to be everywhere at once. Be ubiquitous. Acquire a reputation for bilocation; you want people to say, 'Why, President Smithers, I just don't know you do it. . . .'" or "Find one initiative—say, a new building—to be identified with, and identify yourself with it at every opportunity."

That such simplistic (even cynical) folklore prescriptions should be offered as truths by veteran presidents is evidence of our problem—in thinking about leadership, we are too ready to traffic in imagery, to take appearance for reality.

To be sure, these bad habits are not unique to higher education. In national politics, incumbents are assailed (and then, often, rejected at the polls) simply because they have become incumbents, having lost the pristine luster of candidates. We see President Clinton's ratings climb upward and plunge back down, whipsawed by events (many beyond presidential control), while a file of anonymous Republicans announce their candidacy. The spectacle exerts the same despair-tinged fascination that hooks us into the O.J. Simpson trial. Is this real? Is this us?

It is dangerous to remain in this trance. Our need for effective leadership was never greater, particularly in higher education, whose problems worsen by the year.

How can we enhance the likelihood of successful presidential leadership? First, we need to jettison some illusions and shibboleths about leadership, some half-truths and oversimplifications. We need to deal with the fact that our concept of leadership success is unclear, beclouded as it is by paradox, accident, and aberration.

Presidential Search: Ritual or Science Fiction?

The way we search for presidents is revealing. Outside academe, it is hard to find such an intricate dance with so many partners, such a process-laden, symbol-strewn procedure. Operationally, however, there is nothing wrong with our searches—they work well enough, they do find presidents, and one can imagine other procedures, including more efficient ones, that would be much worse. But it is a peculiar process, and its peculiarities reveal some of the follies in our thinking about presidential leadership.

What is most useful and most delusional about searches comes down to the same thing: They consist of rituals that meet our needs as communities but offer little rational analysis of what is required for leadership success—little basis for predicting it, and less for assuring it. Although the dialogue of the search is often rich, and it does shape the decision, the shaping tends to be symbolic rather than practical. For instance, the process may determine that the next president should be a scholar rather than a financial type, be charismatic rather than bureaucratic, be decisive rather than process-oriented . . . or should be an alum . . . or (although these preferences will not be stated) of a certain religion, race, or gender. Such a preference, legal or not, does reveal how we think about our institutional past and future, and may clarify our values, which is all to the good. But it does not indicate much reflective thinking about what we want the next leader to do, about how institutional success will be enhanced under this leader, about how success will be measured.

Some have noted that a search has a religious function, allowing us to posit the vision of a utopian leader (and thus of the college as a utopia). Updated for the cyber age, a search may be compared to a science-fiction stargate leading to an alternate universe, where the image we project (of ourselves and the leader who will guide us) becomes virtual reality.

Asked to list criteria, committees come up with a composite sketch of a messianic leader who can articulate the true vision of Siwash so that all who hear it will at last understand and believe, be a financial whiz, have knockout interpersonal skills, listen closely, be decisive but open, round up major funding on the way to the interview, and . . . all losses restore and sorrows end.

Unreality increases as the search goes on. A search firm pledges to find the top prospects in the country for this job. Never mind that the top thousand prospects, already presidents, are not available. That the next ten thousand don't want to be a college president (thanks, but they already have jobs—with higher earnings, less aggravation, and more security).

Some good prospects have no interest in moving to Siwash. Some bad ones are interested because they want out of where they are (people can't wait for them to leave, but you won't find this out), or they are looking for a quick stepping stone to somewhere else.

It takes a true believer to imagine this process will discover the one best person for the job, and the one who will solve our problems (problems we find overwhelming). But whether seen as religious rituals or projections of virtual reality, our searches imply that this is exactly what we do believe.

Given their magical quality, perhaps searches are not the best place to look for clear thinking. Let's consider some of the ways in which leadership success is assessed and analyzed in life-after-search—in the tenures of those lucky few who join the ranks of appointed presidents. What makes us consider a given president successful? What indicators or correlations do we use?

First, for some who analyze presidential leadership from a scholarly perspective, success is correlated, logically if somewhat tautologically, with the support on which it is seen to depend. A second correlation, less scholarly but logical enough, is between success and longevity, on the assumption that leaders who keep their jobs are succeeding. A third—if less logical—correlation, sometimes made by search committees and boards, reverses the second, equating success with mobility.

Success and Support: The Three-Legged Stool and Other Parables. It has been argued (by Birnbaum among others) that presidential success depends on a three-legged stool: the support of board, faculty, and executive officers. Although other constituencies are important—students, alumni, staff, community—the support of the first three is fundamental.

But not all sources of support are equal. A strong-minded board, unshakable in its support of a president (or equating a challenge with a threat to its authority), can empower a president to face down a faculty vote of no confidence. However, if a board is determined to remove the president, a faculty can seldom find the will or the way to keep the leader in office. Finally, while the support of senior executives is a mark of lasting presidencies, a variation is the executive team deliberately kept weak as a foil to the CEO.

Although analyzing success in terms of support is a useful frame, it seems to accept the premise that support, staying power, and successful leadership are linked and can be equated. This equation, however, neglects the dramas of power, the aberrations of support, and the ambiguities of long tenures. For instance, long-term leaders may seem to have broader support than they do because dissent has been silenced and critics intimidated. Though many may be dismayed by the leader, expressions of dismay are seldom heard, and no wonder.

On the other hand, a leader may persist despite seeming to lack support in crucial areas. The leader endures a chorus of criticism, year after year, but remains in office. Why? Not only because the leader's accomplishments are substantial, but because the leader does have solid support, in crucial places. It is simply not as visible or audible as the criticism. Just as there are successful leaders who have less support than you might think, there are those with more support than meets the eye.

Take the case of Cito Gaston. (Presidents *are* like baseball managers—they turn over often, are blamed for what they can't control, and are eagerly accepted by other organizations after they've left their last one.) After the

Toronto Blue Jays won their first World Series in 1992, having captured the American League pennant several years in a row, Peter Gammons wrote of their manager, Gaston: "He has finished first three times in four years and yet somehow he has never received public respect. The local hacksaw columnists bash him daily. The local all-sports talk show is even worse . . . and he has been bashed within the organization" (Gammons, 1994).

Why was Gaston considered successful, despite an acute lack of popularity with vocal and influential parts of his constituency? Because of his record, to be sure, but also because he was seen by those who knew him best as a person of fairness and consistency, commanding respect without raising his voice, and bringing out the best in people over the long haul.

Students of presidential leadership will recognize in Gaston the pattern of a quietly competent executive who leads without flash and fanfare, who handles crises calmly, manages pressure well, and supports people in line positions, giving them credit for what they do—a executive with no need to be perceived as superhuman. Such presidents willingly preside over institutions that are not president-centric—that is, where the president has a low profile, and, accordingly, faculty and key executives (provosts, deans) assume greater importance. But how many search committees, intoxicated by the vision of a savior, seriously weigh the benefits of such leadership for their institution, let alone seek it out?

For their part, leaders who embody this approach may do poorly in searches, when they fail to behave as if they had descended from the mountain top with tablets in hand. Such a president, who defines by example one type of success, may become a target for vociferous criticism precisely because of this success, if the community prefers a conventional image of the president-in-charge.

Being There and Staying There: Success and Longevity. As noted, longevity is a fuzzy measure of success. The long-term presidency may be like a happy marriage and a happy family, grounded in a consensus that this arrangement meets everyone's needs. But it can also be the residue of early threats turned aside, a husbanding of support over time, and adroit image management. Closer examination may show the lasting presidency to be an odd conglomerate of igneous and sedimentary histories, of successes and failures: the success of the leader (in weathering storms, staying the course, consolidating power) and the failure of forces that oppose the leader and seek a change. When we judge the president to be a force for the good, we label the opposing forces as chronic malcontents and self-interested grumblers. But what if they represent the more enlightened thinkers on the campus—progressive, thoughtful, concerned for the institution, but powerless to penetrate the closed ranks of president, board, executives?

Are there such examples? Consider the president of a large university who shrugs off two votes of no confidence by the faculty, replaces rebellious board members, deflects investigations by attorney generals, and snarls back at regular thrashings in the press, but who stays in office more than two decades and then proposes to appoint his own successor, without a search. (If such extreme illustrations of leadership aberration did not exist, one would need to invent them.)

Another paradox may be embedded in the amalgam of long-term presidencies: a failure of mobility, that is, the failure of a president to move on at will, though not for lack of trying. Many well-regarded, well-known presidents are on the short list for other positions year after year. The reasons they haven't yet landed the next position, in some cases, can be traced back to peculiarities that give them authority and staying power where they are. Paradoxically, they may appear as all too successful—that is, too identified with particular styles, strategies, and solutions—to be the choice of the next search committee.

Just as myth and image distract us from thinking seriously about leadership, so does a focus on longevity. At one extreme, longevity becomes yet another image that we are too willing to accept on its face value. But the same is true of longevity's flip side, mobility.

Moving On: Mobility as Success. Since the average tenure of a president is now 6.7 years, for every president who lasts for a decade there must be another who leaves after a couple of years. Ironically, among those presidents who move frequently are many regarded as our most successful leaders.

By what standard? By the criteria of prospect-appeal and upward mobility. Here is another case, in which Y is appointed president of a major public university after three years as the system head in another state, preceded by a brief stay in a senior system position in a third state, and before that, a quick turn as president of a prestigious but troubled private college. Through this procession of moves, which took little more than a dozen years to complete, Y has burnished his reputation not only as a perennial top candidate, but as an institutional savior and a troubled-system-transformer.

His stated aspiration as head of the public system just left was to raise its (troubled, disorganized, underfunded) universities to an intellectual level competitive with Berkeley, Santa Cruz, UCLA—an ambition dazzling to some and baffling to others. Its lack of realism may be more apparent in the wake of Y's departure.

Bemused students of Y's trajectory look at the organizations he proposed to transform, noting that their troubles seem unabated. (This can't be laid at Y's doorstep, because the problems were there before he was, but whether anything improved is unclear.) Y's nastiest critics say his speed of foot keeps him one step ahead of trouble. However, with each successive appointment, an organization has found in Y just what it sought, believing that he is the solution to its problems. What is the reality?

This is not so much a riddle as an illustration of two half-truths about leadership.

The first half-truth is called *success-as-reputation*. In this case, success is a kind of shared conclusion based on a set of appearances: perceived potential, acquired visibility, and accreted prestige, multiplied in a mirroring network that validates perceptions. Eventually the perceptions become self-referential determinants of success. It would be overstating the case to say that Y is higher education's answer to Mamie Van Doren: famous for being famous, successful for being successful. But in such a case study we do seem to drift dangerously close to what the French theorist Baudrillard calls *hyper-reality,* where the appearance is the real, where the appointment is, in a virtual sense, a self-defining success, for the individual, whose upward mobility has reached (for now) the top, and for the institution, which believes it has found the best, and the solution to its problems.

The second half-truth is called *success-as-contrast.* Perceptions of success change as people change jobs, and reputations rise and fall with these changes. The conditions of success created by Leader A may not be replicated by B, the successor, and they may also prove difficult for A to reproduce in a new situation.

For instance, to take another case from outside academe, the founding editor of *The New Yorker,* Harold Ross, dreamed of a supreme managing editor who could make his system work perfectly. Although he never found his ideal, he found the next best thing in his successor, William Shawn, who turned an anarchic spill of intuitions, issues, topics, writers, editors, proof readers, fact checkers, typesetters, advertisers, printers, and distributors, into a well-oiled machine that every week produced a product that in its polish and professionalism was a model for its readers, and a model of organization for other editors.

But when the next editor arrived, the machine instantly began to sputter and the network to fray. The system was so much the creation of one person—so strongly identified with him and so linked to his expectations and preferences—that it ceased to be functional when that person was gone. The new editor (himself since replaced) never achieved the reputation of his predecessor. Meanwhile—how things change!—the old editor, though still revered in memory by some, began to be seen by others, in retrospect, as less brilliant than idiosyncratic, once detached from a system that no longer seemed viable. Amazingly enough, a few even began to describe themselves as liberated—from the restrictive, prescriptive, overmanaged process of the once-great editor.

When presidents leave, systems may mysteriously malfunction. Arrangements that worked smoothly for President Old are suddenly creaky and cumbersome for President New. Now they are too convoluted and bureaucratic, where before they seemed like the wheels and springs of a jeweled watch. Or once they seemed models of simplicity, but now they are judged to have been too ad hoc, too seat-of-the-pants, and worse, they seem to have vanished, leaving no record of how things were managed, no institutional history.

Old was surely a success when he was here, the respected captain of a tight ship. But now that New is on board, one sees that trouble was brewing below decks all this time, only battened down and kept out of sight.

Meanwhile, a strange thing happens at the institution recently left by President New, where she was greatly admired. Her systems now seem cumbersome and overcomplicated. In fact, some of her administrative habits (there were those, it turns out, who never really liked them) now seem so dysfunctional that incredulity is openly expressed. How could anyone have managed an organization this way?

For every president Old and New, there is a President Other who is an instant hit just by contrast with a predecessor. President Other wows them with a few quick, no-nonsense decisions, without so much *process*. (What a relief!) Or Other wins friends by introducing a few textbook-simple procedures that seem to bring order to chaos. Or Other delights the faculty just by walking down the hall, a breath of fresh air after years of a CEO whose door was too often closed.

There is a problem here, but it is not Presidents Old, New, and Other. The problem is us. The problem is the knee-jerk superficiality of our shifting perceptions of these presidents as they come and go, our embrace of simplistic concepts of success and failure. We are too ready to praise a newcomer for what is a predictable (and possibly, a manipulated) contrast. We are too eager to fault the previous incumbent for having failed to solve systemic problems (they were there before Old arrived, they will be there when New leaves). We are too eager to focus on what we didn't like about the leadership style of Old, and what we find refreshing in New. We should be focusing on our institutional problems, and how we can work with our leaders to solve them. (The first step is to acknowledge the persistence of the problems; the second step is to realize that they are not the singular problems of Siwash but the social, cultural, and economic problems besetting institutions in the 1990s.) Instead, we react to a moving series of images, like a passive audience in a darkened theater. If presidents turn to image management, perhaps they are only giving us what we have asked for.

Indeed, presidential leadership has acquired some of the slickness of electoral politics, with its image manipulation, its communications specialists, its tracking of positive and negative ratings, its spin control. Thus it is only natural that one of the shibboleths deflecting us from serious thinking about leadership is . . . vision! Like political leaders, all college presidents, Old, New, and Other, are now expected to have *vision* if they are to be considered successful.

The Vision Thing, or What Every Child Expects of a Parent

In its realistic form, a call for vision is a reasonable expectation that a leader can set goals and guide the organization toward a future. In its more outlandish forms, the demand for vision casts the president in the role of a white-robed figure who emerges from the desert with burning eyes and the second sight of a messiah. The visionary leader will see what others have not seen before. Will see, with x-ray vision, the long-hidden archetypal mission of the institution. Will see the future! Will tell us how to get there!

We remember when President Bush, criticized for failing to articulate a vision, began to mutter in Bush-speak about "the vision thing." Some trace his defeat at the polls back to his unwitting derogation of vision. He knew what he was muttering about: President Clinton, elected because someone thought he had more vision, has been attacked for a thousand faults, but for nothing so harshly as for his failure to articulate a clear, consistent vision for the United States.

That we believe such an articulation is possible, and that one person can do it for us, is further evidence that our expectations of leaders are not based on rational thought. It seems that although we cannot think clearly, what we can do is express our anguish in the form of a childish wish that some heroic parental figure will make it all right, make it all go away. This wish shows our longing for certainty, clarity, and a sense of control at a time when these are nowhere to be found.

Are we not powerless against ourselves? We have trashed the earth and abandoned our cities; unleashed a backlash against cures for social ills that remain uncured; fought communism to keep the world safe for a system that apparently doesn't work, since we are getting poorer. No wonder we are looking for someone with a vision of a better future. (And no wonder that some in their desperation turn to messianic zealots, whether in cults or militias.)

We know that higher education is no longer esteemed, and that a public dismayed by our costs and prices holds us accountable for what we seem unable to demonstrate. Thus it is understandable that we ask our leaders to help us restore our sense of primacy, pride, worth—give us back the esprit and morale we once had, when society was convinced of the value of a degree and the prestige of professors. It is understandable, but it is not admirable. And it is dangerous, because the leaders most willing to sound as if they could do this may be, at best, those whose greatest skill is self-presentation. At worst, they will be self-deluded frauds or naked emperors.

The gloomy Baudrillard would contend that such is indeed our fate, that we have already entered hyper-reality where the only leaders are those who dazzle with their visions, their hype, and their upward mobility. In the virtual state, there is never a President Old, only a candidate on the threshold of becoming President New: we have entered the zone where anticipation is experience and image is substance, what Baudrillard calls the "age of simulacra and simulation, in which there is no longer any God . . . nor any last judgment to separate truth from false, the real from its artificial resurrection" (Poster, 1988, p. 142).

Out of the Hyper-Real: Reclaiming Reality

It is up to us, as citizens of our institutions, to demonstrate that this grim scenario is untrue. We can do so by assuming greater collective responsibility for leadership success. This entails being more realistic in our expectations of leaders, and working toward the conditions that allow leaders to succeed. The heart of this project is thinking more seriously about the core tasks of leadership.

The demands of leadership are always formidable. To be realistic about these demands is not to minimize or to lower our expectations of leaders—it is simply to focus those expectations in a more thoughtful way. One could begin with the inescapable components of a president's job (as Mayor Richard Daley put it, "picking up the garbage"—in which he included making sure the traffic lights work, the subways run, the police cars have gas, and so on).

Here is a *Reader's Digest* condensation of the "the garbage" of the president's job—the minimum that any president needs to get done: recruit students, meet the payroll, balance the budget, raise more funds, sustain the academic program, and support the faculty. A leader who can manage these basics will do fairly well, and a president with major problems in a few of these areas over time will not be judged a success.

Say for the sake of the argument that all three thousand or so of our presidents get these jobs done. In other words, assume normal competence. Further assume that ways in which the tasks are done—that is, the leadership styles—and the relative magnitudes and priorities of the tasks, will vary widely across institutional type, size, location, endowment, predicament, history, and stage of development. Assuming commonalties of competence, and allowing for institutional and stylistic differences, what are the characteristics we seek in successful presidential leaders?

Everyone will have a personal list. Here is mine:

Understanding: We should expect our leaders to be intellectuals in the old, affirmative sense of the word, to show scope and curiosity, subtlety and accuracy in their thinking. I would trade a truckload of vision for a vial of true understanding in any president.
Values: The president's values should be humane, progressive, idealistic. Although academic communities mirror the populations they serve, they can also be better than that. Many of the world's movers and shakers are ruthless, vengeful, and abusive, are hysterically competitive and indifferent to whatever does not serve their ends. We can expect academic leaders to conform to a different standard.
Calm: For presidents, the question is not whether crises will arise, or when, but how the president will respond. Communities need to know that their leaders will be calm, steady, and resourceful in a crisis.
Courage: The courage of convictions. The courage to accept criticism. The courage to do the right thing.
Fairness: A sense of integrity and consistency.

Does my list seem to ask too much . . . or too little? (Where are *creative, dynamic, risk-taking, buoyant, visionary?*) I leave the question to the reader, but what I find most striking about my list is that, in its principal points, it will serve equally well as a list of qualities we would be pleased to find in a spouse, parent, or child, in a neighbor, friend, or colleague, in a supervisor, in any member of an administration, staff, or faculty. They are qualities we would happy to discover in (and might well demand from) ourselves.

One way to move out of hyper-reality and back to the real, to escape from superficial thinking about leadership, is to ask of leaders what we expect of ourselves, at best, and to demand of ourselves the same qualities that we expect in our leaders.

What a wonderful starting point for search committees. As they list their criteria, they could ask themselves: Are there many people who fit the profile we have described? (There should be thousands. If there aren't, look into it.) Are the qualities we seek in a leader also qualities we can observe in the people around this table, our own search committee (and if not . . .). We need to take collective responsibility not only for thinking leadership through, but for creating the conditions that allow us to find, support, and keep good leaders. By setting high but realistic standards both for leaders and for ourselves, finally, we will increase the odds for institutional success.

Although I have emphasized the collective responsibility of communities, let me be clear: we do need leaders, and we need good ones—now more than ever. Higher education today is threatened in many ways, inside and out, and if the draconian cuts contemplated by the current Congress become reality, many of us will be teetering on the brink of disaster. We have an urgent need for sound, strong, clear-headed leadership in the presidency. But if we ask for magic, if we ask for mystical visions and control of the uncontrollable, we may get phrase makers and poseurs at best, charlatans and despots at worst. If we ask for intelligence, probity, and courage, we have a better chance of getting good leaders. Asking for the same qualities in ourselves will make it more likely that our leaders and our institutions can succeed.

Postscript: A Personal Report and Some Parting Advice

To conclude, I would like to return to the personal and speak from my own experiences, two of which in particular might be illuminating to new presidents. Let me call them the Tales of Two Wolves.

The first, called "The Wolf in Sheep's Clothing," concerns the way I became a president. I was an academic dean when the state system chancellor asked if I would consider serving as interim president at a state college that had suffered a convulsive transition. One president had come and gone twice in the span of a year and a half—first resigning, then returning after going to court to get the job back, and then resigning again, under fire.

Whatever the rights and wrongs of that tumultuous tale, it left in its wake a college community divided, distrustful, and demoralized. With no heart for another presidential search, they sought an interim figure to calm troubled waters and begin a healing process.

After discussions with trustees, faculty, staff, and students, I took a leave of absence from my job and accepted the invitation to become their interim president.

What happened next was neither predictable nor astonishing: By October, people were wondering aloud if I would be a candidate for the permanent presidency, and by Thanksgiving the chancellor had asked me to consider it. This triggered a process that resembled nothing so much as a four-month on-the-job interview, during which time I was the sole candidate for the position. In March, community and board had determined that they did indeed want me as their president, and in a ceremony notable for its anticlimax, I lost my interim status and became "the president."

One lesson from this unusual process stands out. It is a variation on the proverb that cautions us to be careful what we wish for, in case we get it.

During my lengthy on-the-job scrutiny, the community had a chance to ask questions, week after week, which in conventional searches they would have had less than two days to ask. Several themes emerged (I was asked to state my vision approximately fifty times), but the most important was what I think of as the Wolf in Sheep's Clothing motif.

The community (like all communities when they search?) wanted a president who would stress participation and colleagueship. Apparently I filled the bill. But as conversations went on, some faculty members were mistrustful. If appointed, would I remove my kindlier, gentler disguise and stand revealed as yet another fire-breathing top-down type, a wolf in sheep's clothing?

Two years later, reality and normalcy having long since set in, some faculty and staff seemed bemused by my leadership style, which stressed developing leadership in executive officers, enabling middle managers, delegating broadly, looking to faculty for leadership in curriculum development, and asking the community to work at a sense of common purpose. While many valued this approach, some seemed to wonder why their president wasn't more presidential. It dawned on me that they were comparing me, not with the short-term president whose immediate legacy I inherited, but the president before last. He had been a very effective president of a very particular stripe—top-down, demanding, brisk—unequivocally the chief decision maker, unambiguously the leader in charge. In place of this management style, I had introduced a philosophy of leadership in many ways antithetical.

I concluded that while some appreciated a sheep in sheep's clothing, others perhaps had all along covertly wished for what they professed to fear—a wolf.

If there is advice for a new president based on this experience, it is the advice of Polonius to Hamlet: Be yourself. Be faithful to the leadership style that flows from your temperament and beliefs. But of course, the second piece of advice, which follows naturally, is, be prepared to change. Because things do change. This is the moral of my second tale, called "The Wolf at the Door."

In my fourth year as president, the wolf arrived. For the two previous years, each fall and each spring I had dolefully advised the community that if our economic and demographic circumstances, which were gripping us like a vice, continued to worsen, we would reach a point where belt tightening would no longer be enough, and we would have to reduce personnel. Some, hearing this year after year without observing dire consequences, suspected that I was crying wolf, and speculated as to why. But last January, a midyear drop in enrollment pushed us to the brink, and I saw that we would need to become smaller and more efficient. Not only restructuring but downsizing lay ahead of us, which meant layoffs, the first in the college's history.

To keep this story mercifully short, the process, which took us from January to that dreaded moment in April when layoffs were announced, was one in which in which the burdens of leadership lay squarely at the president's doorstep. And inevitably, as I shouldered the responsibility for decisions that had to be mine, the temperature of many professional and personal relationships cooled. If in reality the wolf at the door was an inexorable combination of economy, demographics, poor state support, insufficient financial aid, and fierce competition, for some the wolf at the door appeared as the president. So be it.

For after all the consultation, delegation, deference and thoughtful process in the world, there are decisions only the president can make, and they must be made. When they are made, many will dislike them. People will be hurt, resentful, angry. They will say things about you that you hope your mother never hears. But if you make the decisions carefully, with clear (even if not shared) rationales, with the good of the institution in mind, your decisions (and you) will eventually be respected.

Make no mistake, this experience will be difficult, and it will be new. Nothing you have done as a faculty member, department chair, or dean really prepares you for it. But if you can see the institution recover from the shocks of downsizing, and accept your decisions as necessary and even appropriate; if you can see the community move on to serious restructuring and discover some of its benefits (greater responsibility and accountability, collaboration and cooperation, efficiency and effectiveness); if you can witness the imagination and creativity that stressful opportunities release in the best people; if you can see the institution strengthened and positioned for the future: then you may experience the gratification that accompanies the responsibility of being a president.

Although it is a job whose perils and pleasures alternate constantly, the presidency can be deeply satisfying. Of course, if you are already a new president, you will have begun to discover this for yourself.

References

Gammons, P. *Boston Globe,* Feb. 27, 1993, sports section.
Poster, M. (ed.). *Jean Baudrillard: Selected Writings.* Stanford, Calif.: Stanford University Press, 1988.

ROBERT HAHN is president of Johnson State College in Johnson, Vermont.

A long-time observer of higher education offers his reflections on the college and university presidency.

Afterword: Reflections on the College Presidency

David Riesman

My interest in the presidency dates back to my days as a student at Harvard College, where I brought college and university presidents to talk to very small groups of undergraduates about their institutions. I brought Clarence Cook Little from the University of Michigan and Hamilton Holt from Rollins College, who helped to create a radical and short-lived college, Black Mountain, in North Carolina. I came to know Harvard's president, A. Lawrence Lowell, when, as editor of the *Harvard Crimson*, I broke the story about his plan to create the residential college system at the college.

When I first entered academic life myself, I made colleges and universities my tribes. Their study did not require learning a new language, or suffering the hazards of fieldwork among preliterate peoples! Robert Hutchins, then director of the Santa Barbara Center, supported by the Ford Foundation, invited me to do an analysis of a study of academic freedom he had commissioned from Columbia University sociologist Paul Lazarsfeld. The venture took me to institutions from the University of Wisconsin, Whitewater, to what is now North Carolina Agricultural and Technical State University. Later, service on the Carnegie Commission of Higher Education, directed by Clark Kerr, introduced me to still a larger range of colleges and universities and presidents.

I never wanted to be a president myself, because I thought the position so onerous, even when it was far more equable than the situation now. From the beginning, I was curious about individuals brave enough to take on the often unanticipated hazards unique to the position of president. I realized that they had to have a certain buoyancy to survive the many assaults upon them, and an ability to focus on the more positive aspects of the job, such as the extraordinary variety of interesting people they get to meet in the course of their work. One of the discoveries many presidents appreciate, for example, is that raising money, far from being an unhappy burden and distraction, is one of the more pleasant parts of the task. It brings them in contact with alumni—and, increasingly, also alumnae—and can be a nice antidote to coping with more individualistic faculty members, who tend to be more pessimistic today.

In my observation, most constituencies most of the time overestimate the power presidents have. State authorities appear to conclude that presidents have too much power, and hence need to be kept on a very short leash, whether of line-item budgets or pre- and post-audits. In many states, open meeting laws require the president to meet with the board of trustees in a glare of publicity on the assumption that if this were not the case, mischief would be done. It is convenient for states to use formula funding to impose a leveling equity on quite disparate academic institutions within the state, and then for state officials to expect the president to maintain morale within the formulae, no matter what the idiosyncracies of the particular institution. It is also convenient for trustees and some state officials to see the president as a chief executive officer who ought to be able to run a tight ship with a minimum of extraneous noise from faculty or students.

Many faculty want to see the president as having authority because they want favors they hope the president will grant, whether to themselves or their department or research institute. They want someone to blame if their expectations are not met. Anyway, the president lives in a bigger house, though it is rarely a home, than do most faculty and has a salary higher than all but the dean and some other people at the medical school—though far less than the total earnings of the professors who may be gene-splicing biologists, macroeconomists, or consultants.

Perhaps the majority of students in a residential institution regard the president as someone they rarely see around the dorms, though they seldom bother to invite him or her, but whom they can attack if the accommodations or food service are not to their liking. They see the president as glorified talk-show host and innkeeper. The activist students, who are often on the student newspaper, want someone they can bang against for what causes have local standing, someone who, as in the late sixties and early seventies, could represent with a semihuman face all that is regarded as hideous in society at large.

Journalists want to see the president as having enough authority to justify the amount of attention they lavish on the external leader, although of course the spotlight differs in terms of its intensity and range from the president of a flagship campus to an urban community college to a small private college in a rural area.

I continue to admire college and university presidents, especially in the present era when there is no authority in the United States that possesses authority, and presidents must secure support both outside and inside their institutions, despite the widespread lack of respect and the enormous fiscal and recruitment problems. I think college presidents today face unprecedented difficulties extramurally and intramurally. I hope that this volume offers support not only to new but to wearied but still energetic presidents, who are in office long enough to be aware of some of the hazards and, happily, not yet or perhaps ever bored with their job.

DAVID RIESMAN *is Henry Ford II Professor of Social Sciences Emeritus at Harvard University.*

INDEX

American Association of University Professors (AAUP), 45
Analogies and stories, 5, 13, 59–61, 82–84
Angell, J., 45
Announcement, president appointment, 62

Bakken, M., 6–7
Baudrillard, M. J., 78, 80
Bender, T., 42
Bensimon, E. M., 11
Boards of trustees and college presidents, 23–24, 34–35, 39, 75; and public speaking, 47–48
Bok, D., 47
Bond issues funding, 29–30
Bornstein, R., 41–48
Botstein, L., 43
Burnout, avoiding, 54

Change: achieving your vision and, 66–69; being prepared for, 83–84; in college presidency roles, 45–47; pace and timing of, 12, 19–20
Cheever, D., 11
College. See Institution
College leadership. See Leadership
College president jobs: complexity of, 45–46, 72; core tasks of, 80–81; fundraising, 86; history of, 41–42, 46–47; longevity of, 5–6, 45, 76–79, and public policy roles, 42–47; and symbolic roles, 8, 19, 43, 44. See also Staff
College president priorities. See Time management
College president selection. See Selection of presidents
College presidents: accessibility of, 61–65, 66; close observation of, 8, 22, 45, 83; comparing, 78–79, 83; early departures by, 9–11; failures of, 9–11; and family issues, 54–55; homes of, 54–55; ideal, 72–73; interim, 81–82; local visibility and recognition of, 8, 16–18, 43; longevity and mobility of, 5–6, 45, 76–79; national visibility and influence of, 44–45; office hours, 63, 66; personal and private issues facing, 43, 51–56, 69, 83; personal values of, 20, 31–32, 65–66, 69, 71–72, 82–84; power of, 18–19, 45, 60–61, 84, 86; qualifications, 72, 74; smooth entries by, 11–13; and the spouse role, 55–56; support for, 75–76; surprises facing new, 7–8; surveys of, 42–44; workshops for, 73. See also New college presidents

Communication: informal consultations, 62–63; modeling, 13, 66–67
Community colleges: city partnership with, 29–30; geographic organization of, 25–27
Comparisons between presidents, 78–79, 83
Constituencies of college presidents, 46, 75, 86; consulting the, 64–65; long-standing needs of, 66–67; participatory planning by all, 67–68; and public policy roles, 42–44. See also Relationship development
Cox, S. A., 25–32, 30

Daley, R., 81
Debate, public, 36–37; survey of president roles in, 42–44
Decision making: as a campuswide process, 36–40; fast-track task force, 66–67; gathering input for, 61–65; lateral, 20; leadership options, 34–36; modeling commitment and, 66–67; president search, 74–75, 81–82; responsibility, 83–84; styles, 82–83. See also Leadership
Diver analogy, 5, 13
Downsizing, 84

Election campaigns: local bond issue, 30; party, 43–44
Eliot, C., 45
Enrollment, declining, 28
Equipment allocation, 28
Evening classes and facilities, 28

Faculty: and the president, 19, 21–23, 45, 75, 86; salaries and benefits, 64–65, 66–67; socializing with, 19
Faculty senate, 34
Failures of presidents, common causes of, 9–11
Family of the president, 54–55
Financial issues: bond issue funding, 29–30; and decision making, 21–22, 64–65; presidential home endowment, 55
Flawn, P. T., 44

Gade, M. L., 45, 46
Gammons, P., 76
Gardner, D., 52
Gaston, C., 75–76
Gaudiani, C., 59–70
Gilmore, T. N., 7
Gordon, M. A., 51–56
Gordon, M. F., 51–56
Governance, college: and decision making,

34–39, 64–65; and faculty, 21–22. *See also* Boards of trustees
Green, M. F., 45
Hahn, R., 71–84
Henderson, C., 45
Hesburgh, T. M., 46
High school buildings, using, 28–29
History: of college president roles, 41–42, 46–47; learning the institution's, 17, 62–63
Holt, H., 85
Home, presidential, 54–55
Honan, W. H., 42
Houston Community College System (HCCS), 25–29
Humor, care in use of, 22
Husband of the president, recognition of, 55–56
Hutchins, R. M., 44, 45, 46, 85

Images of presidents, changing, 75–79
Institution: importance of history and traditions of, 17, 62–63; mismatches between president and, 9–10; and prearrival activities of president, 61–63; space and facilities for an, 27–31; traditions, 17
Intellectuals, public. *See* Public roles of presidents
Interim college presidency, 81–82

Journalists, 86

Kerr, C., 45, 46, 85

Layoffs, personnel, 84
Lazarsfeld, P., 85
Leaders. *See specific names*
Leadership: characteristics of, 81–82; core tasks of, 80–81; encouraging civic, 47–48; ideal, 72–73; irrational expectations of, 79–80; isolation and loneliness of, 19, 22–23, 54; lateral form of, 20; and listening, 62–63; in a "post-heroic age," 45; roles in civic, 43, 44–48; superficial thinking about, 75–79; training, 73. *See also* Decision making
Listening skills, 62–63
Little, C. C., 85
Local community relations, 16, 30
Lowell, A. L., 85

McLaughlin, J. B., 8, 44, 46
Martin, R. H., 15–24
Mayer, M., 44, 46
Meeting people, 16–17, 69
Meetings: formal brainstorming, 64–65; informal consultation, 62–63
Miami Tribe of Oklahoma, 34, 37, 38
Miami University, 33–40
Mobility of college presidents, 5–6, 45, 76–79
Moravian College, 15–24
Myth making, 72

Names, learning people's, 16–17, 69
Names of teams. *See* Team nickname controversy
Native Americans, and team names, 33–34, 36–37, 38
Neutrality, institutional, 44, 47
New college presidents: assumptions of, 15–16; early success by, 67; expectations about, 79–80; first-year journal, 15–24; inaugural address components, 65–66; postinaugural leadership by, 66–69; pre-arrival activities, 61–63; pre-inauguration activities, 64–65; recognition and visibility of, 16–18; surprises facing, 7–8, 17; transition plans of, 11–12, 61–65. *See also* College presidents

Perceptions of presidents, shifting, 75–79
Personal philosophies of college presidents, 20, 31–32, 65–66, 69, 71–72, 82–84
Planning: new president transition, 11–12, 61–65; participatory and comprehensive, 67–68
Police, campus, 17
Politics, partisan, and college presidents, 43–44
Poster, M., 80
Privacy issues, 54–55
Pronouncements. *See* Speech-making
Public roles of presidents, 41; and boards of trustees, 47–48; changing, 45–47; survey on, 42–44. *See also* Speech-making

Reading time, 52–53
Redskin nickname. *See* Team nickname controversy
Reedy, J., 46
Reich, R., 29
Relationship development: with board of trustees, 23–24; with faculty, 21–23; importance of, 12–13, 24; local community, 16, 30; with president's staff, 20–21, 75; with students, 16–17, 18, 86. *See also* Constituencies of college presidents; Staff
Riesman, D., 8, 44, 46, 85–87
Risser, P. G., 8, 33–40
Ross, H., 78
Ross, M., 45
Rothkopf, A., 7

Scapegoating, 10
Scarcella, L., 29–30, 31–32
Selection of presidents: criteria for, 72, 74, 81–82; mistakes in, 9–10; search processes, 74–75, 82–83. *See also* New college presidents
Shawn, W., 78
Shriver, P. R., 34
Silber, J., 45
Software, management, 69
Southwest College, Houston: creation of, 25–26; development of, 27–32

Space: president's home, 54–55; search for campus, 27–31
Speech-making: inauguration address, 65–66; and pronouncements, 18–19, 65; on public issues, 42, 46, 47–48
Spouse of the president, roles and recognition of, 55–56
Stacy, B., 56
Staff: benefits, 66–67; downsizing, 84; listening to, 62–63, 66; president's, 20–21, 75. *See also* Relationship development
Stafford, Texas, 27. *See also* Southwest College, Houston
State authorities, 86
Stone Soup, 59–61
Stories and analogies, 5, 13, 59–61, 82–84
Students, relationships with, 16–17, 18, 86
Success: and longevity, 76–77; and mobility, 77–79; and support, 75–76
Surveys of college presidents, 42–44
Symbolism in president roles, 8, 19, 43, 44
Systematic management systems, 68–69

Team nickname controversy: background, 34–37; decision, 38–39; history, 33–34; and institutional values, 37–38; time devoted to, 36, 39–40

Technology education, 27–28
Thank-you policy, 66
Time management: and demands, 7, 45–46, 51–52; office hours, 63, 66; scheduling and personal, 52–54; and setting priorities, 12, 48; systematic, 68–69; and value conflicts, 36, 39–40. *See also* College president jobs
Traditions, institutional, 17
Transition plans, new president, 11–12, 61–65
Trustees. *See* Boards of trustees

Vacation and private time, 53–54
Value conflicts case study: decision discussion, 38–39; decision process, 36–37; history and background, 33–37; and institutional values, 37–38; a president's dilemma, 34–37; time cost, 36, 39–40
Values of college presidents, personal, 20, 31–32, 65–66, 69, 71–72, 82–84
Vision setting by a president, 59–61, 70; expectations of, 79–80; inauguration address, 65–66; postinaugural, 66–69; pre-arrival, 61–63; pre-inauguration, 64–65

Wife of the president, recognition of, 55–56
"Wolf at the Door" story, 83–84
"Wolf in Sheep's Clothing" story, 82–83

Ordering Information

NEW DIRECTIONS FOR HIGHER EDUCATION is a series of paperback books that provides timely information and authoritative advice about major issues and administrative problems confronting every institution. Books in the series are published quarterly in Spring, Summer, Fall, and Winter and are available for purchase by subscription and individually.

SUBSCRIPTIONS for 1996 cost $50.00 for individuals (a savings of 34 percent over single-copy prices) and $72.00 for institutions, agencies, and libraries. Standing orders are accepted. New York residents, add local tax for subscriptions. (For subscriptions outside the United States, add $7.00 for shipping via surface mail or $25.00 for air mail. Orders *must be prepaid* in U.S. dollars by check drawn on a U.S. bank or charged to VISA, MasterCard, or American Express.)

SINGLE COPIES cost $19.00 plus shipping (see below) when payment accompanies order. California, New Jersey, New York, and Washington, D.C., residents, please include appropriate sales tax. Canadian residents, add GST and any local taxes. Billed orders will be charged shipping and handling. No billed shipments to post office boxes. (Orders from outside the United States *must be prepaid* in U.S. dollars by check drawn on a U.S. bank or charged to VISA, MasterCard, or American Express.)

SHIPPING (SINGLE COPIES ONLY): one issue, add $5.00; two issues, add $6.00; three issues, add $7.00; four to five issues, add $8.00; six to seven issues, add $9.00; eight or more issues, add $12.00.

DISCOUNTS FOR QUANTITY ORDERS are available. Please write to the address below for information.

ALL ORDERS must include either the name of an individual or an official purchase order number. Please submit your order as follows:
  Subscriptions: specify series and year subscription is to begin
  Single copies: include individual title code (such as HE82)

MAIL ALL ORDERS TO:
  Jossey-Bass Publishers
  350 Sansome Street
  San Francisco, California 94104-1342

FOR SUBSCRIPTION SALES OUTSIDE OF THE UNITED STATES, contact any international subscription agency or Jossey-Bass directly.

AVAILABLE
HIGHER E...RIES
Martin ...mer, Editor-in-Chief

- E92 Conflict Management in Higher Education, *Susan A Holton*
- E91 Assessing Performance in an Age of Accountability: Case Studies, *Gerald H. Gaither*
- E90 Information Technology and the Remaking of the University Library, *Beverly P. Lynch*
- E89 Rethinking Tuition and Student Aid Strategies, *Edward P. St. John*
- E88 Academic Freedom: An Everyday Concern, *Ernst Benjamin, Donald R. Wagner*
- HE87 Developing Administrative Excellence: Creating a Culture of Leadership, *Sharon A. McDade, Phyllis H. Lewis*
- HE86 Total Quality Management on Campus: Is It Worth Doing? *Daniel Seymour*
- HE85 America's Investment in Liberal Education, *David H. Finifter, Arthur M. Hauptman*
- HE84 Strengthening the College Major, *Carol Geary Schneider, William Scott Green*
- HE83 Financial Management: Progress and Challenges, *William E. Vandament, Dennis P. Jones*
- HE82 Important Lessons from Innovative Colleges and Universities, *V. Ray Cardozier*
- HE81 Recognizing Faculty Work: Reward Systems for the Year 2000, *Robert M. Diamond, Bronwyn E. Adam*
- HE80 Assessment and Curriculum Reform, *James L. Ratcliff*
- HE79 Agendas for Church-Related Colleges and Universities, *David S. Guthrie, Richard L. Noftzger, Jr.*
- HE78 Information Literacy: Developing Students as Independent Learners, *D. W. Farmer, Terrence F. Mech*
- HE77 The Campus and Environmental Responsibility, *David J. Eagan, David W. Orr*
- HE76 Administration as a Profession, *Jonathan D. Fife, Lester F. Goodchild*
- HE75 Faculty in Governance: The Role of Senates and Joint Committees in Academic Decision Making, *Robert Birnbaum*
- HE74 The Changing Dimensions of Student Aid, *Jamie P. Merisotis*
- HE73 Using Consultants Successfully, *Jon F. Wergin*
- HE72 Administrative Careers and the Marketplace, *Kathryn M. Moore, Susan B. Twombly*
- HE71 Managing Change in Higher Education, *Douglas W. Steeples*
- HE70 An Agenda for the New Decade, *Larry W. Jones, Franz A. Nowotny*
- HE69 Financial Planning Under Economic Uncertainty, *Richard E. Anderson, Joel W. Meyerson*
- HE67 Achieving Assessment Goals Using Evaluation Techniques, *Peter J. Gray*
- HE64 Successful Strategic Planning: Case Studies, *Douglas W. Steeples*
- HE62 Making Computers Work for Administrators, *Kenneth C. Green, Steven W. Gilbert*
- HE61 Leaders on Leadership: The College Presidency, *James L. Fisher, Martha W. Tack*
- HE60 Increasing Retention: Academic and Student Affairs Administrators in Partnership, *Martha McGinty Stodt, William M. Klepper*
- HE59 Student Outcomes Assessment: What Institutions Stand to Gain, *Diane F. Halpern*
- HE45 Women in Higher Education Administration, *Adrian Tinsley, Cynthia Secor, Sheila Kaplan*